D0065997

The Kingdom of Love and Knowledge

A. M. ALLCHIN

THE KINGDOM OF LOVE
AND KNOWLEDGE

*The Encounter between Orthodoxy
and the West*

1982
The Seabury Press
815 Second Avenue
New York, N.Y. 10017

Library of Congress Cataloging in Publication Data

Allchin, A. M.
The kingdom of love and knowledge.

Includes bibliographical references and index.
1. Theology, Eastern church—Addresses, essays,
lectures. 2. Theology, Anglican—Addresses, essays,
lectures. 3. Theology—20th century—Addresses,
essays, lectures. 4. Church of England—Addresses,
essays, lectures. I. Title.
BX325.A44   1982   230   81-8995
ISBN 0-8164-0532-8   AACR2

for

VLADIMIR LOSSKY

theologian

8 June 1903 – 7 February 1958

Contents

IV
THEOLOGIANS OF LOVE AND KNOWLEDGE

Acknowledgements

Of the essays collected in this book, Chapters 5, 7 and 8 have not previously been published. Chapter 1 was first published in *One in Christ*; Chapters 2, 9, 10 and 12 were first published in *Theology*; Chapters 3, 4 and 12 in *Christian*; and Chapters 6 and 11 in *Sobornost*.

The author is grateful to the following for permission to publish extracts from copyright sources:

James Clarke & Co. Ltd: *The Mystical Theology of the Early Church* by Vladimir Lossky.

Dimension Books Inc: *St Symeon's Hymns of Divine Love,* translated by G. A. Maloney, S. J.

The Editor: *Le Messager de L'Exarchat du Patriarche de Moscou et de Toute la Russie en Europe Occidentale*: Special Lossky memorial number of *Le Messager*, nos. 30–31, 1959.

SCM Press Ltd: *The Contradiction of Christianity* by David Jenkins.

The Society for Promoting Christian Knowledge: *The Lambeth Conference Report 1968.*

Yale University Press: *Negative Capability* by N. Scott.

Introduction

I

This book is made up of four sections. Of the essays which it contains many have been published before as separate articles, but most have been revised, some considerably, for inclusion in this collection. They represent an attempt to say something about the nature of theology—how it is possible to think and speak about God in the late twentieth century. They all derive, some more directly, some less, from the meeting between Eastern Orthodoxy and the Christian West. Concerned for the most part with Western writers and Western problems, they seek to see them in relation to the older and larger tradition of the first thousand years of Christian history, and to the continuing, but still largely unknown, tradition of the Christian East. Without a knowledge of this, many of the familiar features of our Western situation can scarcely be understood. The failure to see these questions in a sufficiently broad context can often lead us to an impasse. The book, therefore, represents a small contribution to the bringing into consciousness of large areas of our common Christian heritage, which have been for the most part forgotten, to our own great hurt.

The first section looks at the crisis in Christian thinking and living which has been taking place during the last thirty years. This is a crisis which has been felt on the one side as involving the breakdown of institutions, and the failure of traditional structures of authority in matters both of belief and conduct. We have seen the

growing secularisation of our society. On the other side the same
events have been experienced in terms of 'the death of God', and 'the
coming of age of man'. These phrases, commonly used in the sixties,
already begin to sound dated. We seem to be entering a new situation, and it is the argument of the first part of the book that the
witness of Eastern Orthodoxy has a vital part to play in understanding it. In its insistence that nothing adequate to the being of God
can be said at all, i.e. the apophatic or negative aspect of its tradition, Orthodoxy has, paradoxically, the clue to the making of life-
giving rather than death-dealing affirmations about God—Father,
Son and Holy Spirit. Because they do not seek to define or confine
the deity in words, these affirmations can liberate man, making it
possible for him to enter into the operations of God's grace which
transform and fulfil man's nature. These affirmations seek always to
recognise the utter mysteriousness of all that we can say about God.
They spring from a union of love and knowledge in which men and
women are taken out of themselves, transcend their own limitations,
in a movement of praise and adoration, which enlarges and transforms their capacities of seeing and knowing, as well as of loving and
acting.

The second section of the book contains studies of three
theologians from varied moments in the Church's history: eleventh-
century Constantinople, eighteenth-century Wales, nineteenth-
century Denmark. In all three we are able to see a little of what this
living and life-giving theology implies. All three, it will be noted,
lay great stress on the importance of Trinitarian doctrine and understanding, and in particular on the understanding and experience of
the Holy Spirit. The fact that none of the three is well known in the
English-speaking world should not lead us into the parochialism of
imagining that they are of peripheral importance only. Symeon is
without question amongst the greatest of Christian mystical writers,
a fact which is coming to be widely recognised. Ann has always been
acknowledged within her own tradition as a writer of exceptional
quality, in spite of her having written so little. The interest aroused
in 1976 by the bicentennial celebrations of her birth, showed how
relevant her work still is today. As to Grundtvig, he is arguably the
most influential figure in the whole of nineteenth-century Danish
history. He deserves to be as widely known as his equally great but

totally different compatriot and contemporary, Kierkegaard. In this section we see something of the content of the faith, as known in life, in a union of love and knowledge.

In the third section we are more concerned with the given structures of faith, worship and ministerial order, as they are seen from a point of view within the Anglican tradition. It is important to remember that, though it is shaped by certain specific historical experiences, and marked by very clear human and national limitations, this tradition has always claimed to have no specific doctrines, sacraments or church order of its own. It seeks simply to maintain and live by that which it has received from the whole Christian tradition; it seeks, in a situation marked by the bitterness of Christian division and dislocation, to find ways of reconciliation between the East and West in Christendom, no less than between the Churches of the Reformation and Rome. The first and last chapters in this section spring directly out of the work of Anglican-Orthodox dialogue. The first was originally delivered in the Orthodox Theological Institute in Bucharest. The final chapter formed part of the material prepared by the Anglican members of the International Anglican-Orthodox Joint Doctrinal Commission at the opening of their work in 1973; as such it reflects not only the thinking of its author, but long and searching discussion by a representative group of Anglicans from different parts of the world. In the whole of this section less is said about inner experience, more about what is objectively there, given, handed on. We see here more of the shape of the divine initiative which makes possible, in all the frailty of human history, personal and social, a true response of love and knowledge.

The final section of the book looks at three theologians, two Anglican and one Orthodox, who have, in very different ways, achieved this balance of inner and outer, of experience and tradition, and who have in themselves embodied something of the fullness of the mystery of human life, when, in Christ and the Spirit, it is being restored and renewed in the love and knowledge of God. The last essay in the book ought possibly to be read first. It acknowledges a debt which is all-pervasive. The influence of Vladimir Lossky runs throughout the whole, and though perhaps he would not have approved of all the book's conclusions, I hope that he would have recognised in it a desire to remain true to the reality and the tradition which he presented so vividly both in his thinking and in his life.

II

What is it in the theology of Vladimir Lossky which makes his thinking so powerful and creative? It is, and it was for me thirty years ago when I first read his work and had the even greater good fortune to come to know him personally, the vision of a wholly new possibility of what theology can be. It is a vision which opens out new perspectives and possibilities in human life and thought. Old words which have acquired such false meanings as to be no longer usable, 'salvation', for instance, or 'churchman', are suddenly restored to their true significance.

In particular his work clearly reveals the idolatrous nature of much of what has passed for Christian theism. As David Jenkins puts it in another context: 'It is not that God cannot be believed in, but that in much at any rate of Western Christian theism, he has as a matter of fact not been believed in.' In an article published in a short-lived Oxford periodical almost thirty years ago, which everywhere reflects the influence of Lossky's thought, I wrote:

Ever since the development of later scholasticism in the Middle Ages, we have been faced with a false dichotomy between two types of language about God, the mystical and the theological, between the action of the mind and the action of the heart and will in the apprehension of religious truth. The mystics, escaping from the framework of revealed theology and failing to live in the common life of the Church have been unable to communicate their experience to others, so that we reach the present situation in which mystical experience is dismissed as essentially private and incommunicable. On the other hand, the theologians, neglecting the truth that the knowledge of God demands the assent of heart and will as well as of the intellect, have lost the sense of the mystical nature of all theology. They have wished too often to reply to the philosophers on their own ground, and in so doing have laid their theology open to a well-merited philosophical refutation.

To quote David Jenkins again, we have wanted to be sure of God, to 'prove' his existence in a wrong way, 'a way which will enable us to make use of him, or to speak dominatingly or condescendingly of him to others'. As soon as we do this, theological language begins to go bad on us, to lose its true content and significance. For it is a language which must be rooted in the experience and reality of worship in which we put ourselves unconditionally at the disposition of God, and which must be indissolubly linked with an attitude of respect and service towards our fellow human beings and towards all creation. In order to be secure in our own position we have looked for external guarantees of that which must necessarily be its own guarantee.

It has been this development which has tended to make of our talk about God an idol which masks and obscures the reality it speaks about, and which turns men away from the source of life, rather than pointing them towards it. It is this which is at the root of the apostasy of the West.

And not only that, the idol which post-Reformation Christianity, both Catholic and Protestant, has made for itself in the place of God, still has a deadening effect on the Church itself. The essentially religious nature of atheist humanism is derived from this fact; it is a passionate denial and rejection of those images which the Church has, since the Reformation, put before the world, instead of allowing the revelation of God to appear. It is . . . nearer to Christian faith in its rejection of theological idols, than the Church which created them. Here is the explanation of the fact that it is those outside the Churches, or at any rate those who denied what they believed to be traditional Christian belief, who have often played the most Christian role in the last two centuries.

One could give as examples the action of Voltaire in the case of the Calas family, or the work of the Quakers in prison reform in Great Britain. But examples could be multiplied indefinitely.

This is the God, whose death Nietzsche proclaimed nearly one hundred years ago, the news of whose demise has been reaching the general public in these last years.

It has been good for theology, that the astronomers have swept the skies and found no heaven, that the surgeons have dissected the body and found no soul, and that the philosophers have found no place for God as an object of human knowledge. For God, as the great Christian theologians and saints, and particularly those who formed the classical statements of belief, the Creeds, always knew, is neither a philosophical concept nor an object of knowledge. It is he who has made us, and not we him, and it is he who chooses and knows us before ever we can know him. Only in the light of God's complete transcendence of human knowledge, can the idea of Christian revelation, and the nature of theological knowledge be understood, only then can we see, as F. D. Maurice pointed out, that the Divine Name is not a doctrine which we hold, but a reality which upholds us.[1]

The name of F. D. Maurice may well suggest to Anglicans that they have at the heart of their tradition certain hints and suggestions of the way forward to which too little attention has been given. It will also serve to remind us that the debate about God is always and inseparably a debate about man, for there were few theologians in the nineteenth century whose work was more consistently informed with a concern for the common life of all his contemporaries. The contemporary French Orthodox theologian, Olivier Clement, speaks in more than one place of the thirst for a living knowledge of the Trinity, and of the need of our age for a truly Trinitarian paternity, a 'fatherhood lived in brotherly respect for the other so that the life-giving Spirit may be communicated' so that man may be set free to grow into the true dimensions of human existence. Reading such words an Anglican reader can hardly help but think of F. D. Maurice and his great, life-giving discovery of the Name of the Trinity almost a century and a half ago. We may remember the most moving letter in which he explains to his father, a Unitarian minister, how it was that he had come to seek baptism into that Name. We may think of a lifetime of theological writing and reflection, so strangely fruitful in many fields besides theology, in education and literature, in social reform or the emancipation of women, and in the very beginnings of a Christian socialism.

For Maurice the revelation of the Name of God was the foundation of all society amongst men and of all true life within man.

> In asserting the doctrine of the Atonement, we assert redemption, liberty for mankind, union with God, union with each other. . . . When we assert the doctrine of the Trinity, we do so because we believe it to be the grand foundation of all society, the only ground of universal fellowship, the only idea of a God of love. . . . All we want is to maintain a principle without which, we say, men would be divided from each other; a principle which, while we maintain it enables us to claim fellowship with every man who will not disclaim it with us. For the sake of the poor man—for the sake of the denier of these truths . . . we assert and uphold them; for we find them to be the keynotes to all the harmonies of the world, and that without them, all would be broken and dissonant.[2]

To quote F. D. Maurice, in this way, is in itself enough to show that the question in hand is not at all one of simply setting East against West, as though all the truth were on one side, and all the error on the other. The theology of the Eastern Orthodox Churches during the last three or four centuries has certainly not altogether escaped the influences of which we have spoken. All the Orthodox Churches have known their own types of theological academicism, of lifeless scholasticism. Indeed it is only recently that the deadening grip of such a theology on the university faculties in Greece has begun to loosen. In the West, on the other hand, the life-giving knowledge of the Trinity has never ceased to well up within the Church, through the prayer and faithfulness of the Christian people, and especially through the continued reality of the liturgy and the celebration of the sacraments. As F. D. Maurice and Grundtvig both delighted to point out, God has continued to proclaim the Good News at the font and the altar, even when men have been darkening counsel in the pulpit. Everything points to the conclusion that the renewal of Christian vision at the present time, will demand the collaboration of Christian East and West alike, and that this renewal will be very far from a return to the past. Rather it will involve a new apprehension of the faith that all men are one man in Christ Jesus, and that through him in the power of the Spirit, the life of every man can be liberated into the dimensions of God.

For it is the future of *man* which is at stake in the debate about God. If the idol, the 'sadistic father', Nobodaddy, has almost killed man, deprived him of his proper freedom, his authentic joy, so that man has had in turn to overthrow the idol, it is only the discovery of the reality which the image masks, that can make man truly free. For how can man become himself without the knowledge of the Father who gives himself wholly in the Son, who imparts the Spirit, the Spirit of liberty and fulfilment? In a University sermon, preached in Oxford in the autumn of 1967, Metropolitan Anthony Bloom spoke of these things, with the authority which comes to one in whom that liberating fatherhood makes itself known. At its end he declared:

> Our solidarity must be with Christ first, and in him with all men to the last point, to the full measure of life and death. Only then, if we accept this, can we, each of us, and can the congregation of all faithful people, the people of God, grow into what it was in Christ, and what it was in the Apostles, into a group of people whose vision was greater than the vision of the world, whose scope was greater than the scope of the world, so that the Church in the beginning ... could be partaker in all that pertains to the condition of man, and therefore could lead mankind into salvation. And this is not the state in which we are. We have grown small because we have made our God into an idol and ourselves into slaves. We must recover the sense of the greatness of that God revealed in Christ, and the greatness of man revealed by him. And then the world may begin to believe and we may become co-workers with God for the salvation of all things.[3]

NOTES

1. A. M. Allchin. 'The Fallen Idol', *University, A Journal of Enquiry*, Vol II, No. 2, Spring 1952, pp. 45–8

2. Quoted from the first, 1838, edition of 'The Kingdom of Christ', *An Introduction to F. D. Maurice's Theology*, by W. Merlin Davies. London, 1964, p. 27

3. Metropolitan Anthony. 'The True Worth of Man', *Sobornost*, Series 5, No. 6, Winter-Spring 1968, p. 391

I

BEYOND IDOLS

1

Orthodoxy and the Debate about God

It is now fifteen years since a book was published which more than
any other brought theological questions into public debate throughout the English-speaking world, John Robinson's *Honest to God*.
This is not the place to ask why this particular book should have had
so great an effect, and caused a storm which surprised its author as
much as anyone else. Here we simply note the phenomenon, and
remark on the fact that out of the ensuing discussion there has come
a continuing debate about fundamental questions of theology. Can
we know God at all, and if so how? Is it possible to maintain the
traditional Christian affirmations that in Jesus we find true God and
true man? What kind of relationship can there be between the
Judaeo-Christian tradition with its apparently exclusive claims, and
the other religious traditions of mankind? The questions which
occupied so much attention in the earlier part of this century, questions about the nature of the Church and the authority of its ministry, about the understanding of the Church's sacraments, have been
in the last fifteen years seen increasingly as secondary, even though
important, in relation to these greater and more all-embracing
themes.

It is the contention of this essay and of those that follow it, that
the Eastern Orthodox contribution to this discussion is more important than is commonly recognised and that there are basic differences, at least of emphasis, between Christian East and West in
these areas, which give to the Orthodox approach its own specific
character and insight. It is also its contention that the Eastern

Churches cannot, even if they would, insulate themselves from this continuing controversy. For the basic problems which give rise to the debate, particularly the common view of what constitutes valid and valuable knowledge, itself resulting from the development of the scientific view of nature and man, press upon Eastern Christendom no less than on Christians in the West. Man's awareness of himself and of the world in which he is living is undergoing profound modification. And this is not only a Western phenomenon, even though it may have specifically Western roots.

In one of the more permanently valuable books written in the earlier stages of the discussion, David Jenkins argues that our particularly acute Western difficulties about the approach to God have their origin in developments in the Western Christian way of speaking and thinking about God: 'I would argue that what the debate about God particularly shows us is not that God cannot be believed in, but that in much at any rate of Western Christian theism, he has as a matter of fact not been believed in.'[1] He has not been believed in, because what was spoken of in much Western theological writing under the name of God was something or someone less than the living God of the Bible and Christian tradition, the God who is made known to the believer in faith, obedience and worship. God seems to have been reduced to the status of an object of human knowledge, or a concept which we can manipulate or control. Here certainly is one of the reasons why so large a part of the Western world has rebelled against the idea of God altogether. For if there be a God, this cannot possibly be he. Within the development of Protestantism this tendency was one of the factors which led to the Pietist movement with its stress on a religion of the heart, and not of the head; and this movement had a deep influence on the theology of Schleiermacher, and his theory of man's feeling of absolute dependence, as the place where God is to be known.

> Schleiermacher was surely right in being clear that the God with whom Christianity is concerned is not to be equated with that which rounds off a scientific view of the universe, and that which provides a basis for our moral understanding. There is nothing godlike about such a derived object.[2]

But it is precisely with such an object that much Western theology seems to have been concerned. This is particularly true since the end of the sixteenth century. We cannot over-estimate the damage done to our whole understanding of what knowledge of God is, and what it is for, by the exigences of polemic and controversy. God's revelation of himself has been treated not as a transcendent gift to man, given for the healing and restoration of human life, but as the possession of a particular group of men, a weapon to be used for the annihilation of their opponents. This has made us sure of God in quite a false way, sure of him as though we owned him, not as though he held us and all men in his hand. Hence, tragically and too often, God *has* been thought of 'in a way which will enable those who acknowledge him, to be sure of him in a way which will enable them to make use of him, or to speak dominatingly or condescendingly of him to others.'[3] But for Christians to speak of God in such a way, whether amongst themselves, or in their meeting with men of other faiths or none, is at once to falsify the message that they are trying to convey. Thus true words have frequently come to convey false meanings.

But it is not only this polemical quality of much of our theological writing, this habit of holding doctrines *against* others, rather than for the sake of the truth they express, which has warped and vitiated our language about God. There is something deeper and more complex than this; a divorce of systematic theology, of reflection on the Christian mystery, from prayer and silence and worship, which goes back into the centuries before the Reformation. It is this which has led to the separation between the inner, personal experience of the faith, and the outward structures of the Church and of belief, a separation which has been characteristic in different ways of Catholicism and Protestantism alike. It is not that devotion and mystical experience have been absent from Western Christendom. There are countless examples, the great mystics of Spain and France, the founders of Methodism or Pietism, to show that this is not so. But all this inner experience has no longer been integrated into the whole corpus of Christian living and thinking; it has no longer fed and inspired the development of man's reflection on the mystery of God as revealed in Christ. In Catholicism 'mystical theology' has been thought of as a very specialised branch of theological study. In

Protestantism it has virtually ceased to exist. Prayer and devotion have been considered almost optional extras to the development of theological thought. But it is precisely in these things that we come to understand something of the 'Godness' of God, his utter transcendence, his unique and personal manner of meeting with man, his immanence at the heart of man's being. It is in these things that man's 'feeling of absolute dependence' of awe and adoration grows, so that his sense that God cannot be used by him, encompassed and controlled by him, becomes the basis of his thinking about God, the pre-supposition of all his theological reflection.

Thus this element of inner, personal experience is vital. It reveals to us the givenness of God. 'Of the true God there must be some direct awareness which serves somehow to put us on to that unique dimension which is the truly unique dimension of the truly unique God.'[4] But this emphasis on experience is somehow treacherous; it can easily betray the very thing that it is intended to safeguard, turning over into its opposite, and leaving us not with an utterly transcendent God, but with the investigation of our own religious feelings. This weakness is seen above all when experience is taken in isolation. Schleiermacher was surely right, as David Jenkins maintains, to emphasise 'the central importance of the inward experience of the believer'. He was mistaken in taking this point in isolation. '*Sole* emphasis on this, as I have already hinted . . . is a mistake. *Some* emphasis on this, is, I am sure, essential.'[5] From this exclusive emphasis on the world of man's experience there have come incalculable consequences not only for theology, but for the whole life and development of Protestantism.

But now it is at precisely this point that the tradition of the Eastern Church presents us with a very different pattern of understanding, seeming to combine the element of personal experience with that of a shared and common life of faith in a way that is characteristic neither of Protestantism or Roman Catholicism. This can be seen very clearly in a book like Vladimir Lossky's *The Mystical Theology of the Eastern Church*, which, although it was written over thirty years ago, seems at times to have been directly intended for our present situation. It represents a tradition of thinking—and there are few theologians who are more genuinely and freely rooted in the tradition of their Church than Lossky—which steadfastly refuses to make the disjunction of inner and outer, of individual and community with which we are so familiar in the West.

> The Eastern tradition has never made a sharp distinction between mysticism and theology, between personal experience of the divine mysteries and the dogma affirmed by the Church . . . We must live the dogma expressing a revealed truth . . . in such a fashion that instead of assimilating the mystery to our mode of understanding, we should, on the contrary, look for a profound change, an inner transformation of spirit, enabling us to experience it mystically. Far from being mutually opposed, theology and mysticism support and complete each other. One is impossible without the other. If the mystical experience is a personal working-out of the content of the common faith, theology is an expression for the profit of all of that which can be experienced by everyone.[6]

It is vital of course to realise that Lossky does not by 'mystical experience' refer to some esoteric experiences available only to a few special cloistered souls—he was himself married and a layman—but to that common Christian experience of the mysteries of faith, which is open in some degree to everyone who believes.

This experience, this knowledge of God demands of the believer a radical change of heart, which is also a radical change of mind. He must be prepared to think new things, to see new things, to go beyond the normal structures of human thought and knowledge. This is a theme which Lossky constantly stresses. He speaks of the apophatic character of Orthodox theology, its fundamental awareness that God goes beyond all the concepts that we can form of him, and consequently in his revelation of himself to us is all the time calling us to re-form our habitual ways of thinking.

> Such an attitude utterly excludes all abstract and purely intellectual theology which would adapt the mysteries of the wisdom of God to human ways of thought. It is an existential attitude which involves the whole man; there is no theology apart from experience; it is necessary to change, and to become a new man. To know God one must draw near him. No one who does not follow

the path of union with God can be a theologian . . . He who in following this path imagines at a given moment that he has known what God is has a depraved mind, according to St Gregory Nazianzen. Apophaticism is, therefore, a criterion; the sure sign of an attitude of mind conformed to the truth.[7]

This is a point on which David Jenkins also insists, when he points out that if God is God, then his revelation of himself must involve a re-shaping of man's ways of thinking about him. This is a view which at first sight is very difficult for our world to accept. Since the primary model of worthwhile knowing at the present day is provided by the natural sciences, in which it is man who controls, analyses, changes his environment, it is difficult to allow for the possibility of that being real knowledge, where man is less the knower than the known. We shall come back to this point later.

But this experience of God, while it is highly personal, is not, in the Eastern understanding of it, individual. The experience, the knowledge is not given to one man in isolation, but to all together. Only in the community of the common faith, can each one receive the unique vision which is his. The Church as safeguarding, keeping the faith, is not important in Eastern tradition as an infallible institution to which the individual submits, and behind which he can shelter. To think in such a way would derogate from the dignity which God has given man, from his freedom in the Holy Spirit. The Church is, however, important as a network of personal relationships, a shared experience of faith and love and worship; where we can meet one another, and in that meeting, meet God. For the Eastern Orthodox the command to mutual love is inescapably bound up with the perception of the truth of God. In the words which are said in the liturgy before the recitation of the Creed: 'Let us have love one towards another, *so that* with one mind we may acknowledge the Father, the Son and the Holy Spirit, consubstantial, undivided Trinity.' It seems as though our ways of thinking about God are more deeply influenced by our ways of approaching him in worship than we often realise. Certainly one whose central experience of worship is that of a social act, in which he is brought into close relationship with others, in which symbolic gesture is as important as symbolic speech, in which the material things of man's life, real bread and real wine are employed, will feel differently towards God, and have a different understanding of the way in which God discloses himself through social relationships and material things, than someone with quite another practical experience of worship. It is striking on the Protestant side, how behind much of the thought of the great theologians of the last two centuries, there seems to stand the image and the experience of an individual listening to a sermon. Man is addressed by the Word of God; he responds with the decision of faith. It is therefore the liturgical framework in which the experience of each believer is set—and we must remember that in the East 'sacraments' are 'mysteries', and 'sacramental experience' is thus 'mystical experience'—which itself makes, or fails to make, the links between inner and outer; between inner experience and social existence, between personal insight and the whole material cosmos. Our way of thinking about God, and of believing in him is rooted in our approach to him in worship.

But the importance of this social context of the experience, in no way takes away from its uniquely personal nature. It stands in its own right, and can have no final guarantees. This is one of the places where, in David Jenkins's view, the sometimes ambiguous formulae of Schleiermacher

draw attention to an essential element in the knowledge of God which has always been present within the biblical and Christian understanding of theism. It is this—that *the authenticating knowledge of God is not derived but direct.* By 'authenticating knowledge' I mean that knowing which, in the very experiencing of the knower, carries in that experience the assurance that it is indeed knowledge; i.e. that that which is thought to be being known is truly 'there' and is truly being known. Hence it is not 'derived' but 'direct'. One does not infer, or suppose, or even believe, that God exists (however proper or possible those operations may be in their place). God is known to one as existing. (I do not say that God is known *in his* existence because, according to this tradition, the totality of what is truly involved in God's being God is quite beyond human knowing: direct knowledge of God in no way implies total knowledge of God.) This is simply to bring out the implications of the fact that the biblical and Christian tradition of theism has always understood itself as having its ultimate basis both as a matter of fact and as a necessary matter of theory in revelation. The 'godness' of God makes it absolutely inevitable that the only way of being sure (i.e. having knowledge) that God exists lies in God's revealing himself (i.e. in God's making it possible for man to 'come up against him' directly).[8]

The way of expression may differ from that of a writer like Lossky, but there is a striking identity in the substance of what is being said. 'Truth can have no external criterion for it is manifest of itself and made inwardly plain.'[9] The words of Scripture, the decisions of the Councils, the writings of the Fathers, the experience of the saints: these are all things which have a great weight of authority in the Orthodox tradition, and the Eastern theologian will generally tend to take a more 'conservative', less critical attitude towards them than his Western counterpart might do. But they are none of them infallible guarantees. The search for an absolute and infallible authority outside God himself (whether in the Church or in the Bible) seems from the point of view of the Eastern tradition to imply a lack of faith in God and a failure to understand God's respect for man's freedom, and for the way in which the Holy Spirit fulfils and does not destroy the aspiration of man.

But is it not possible to say more of the nature of this 'direct' and self-authenticating experience? Is it possible in a world which takes natural scientific knowledge as the supreme example of worthwhile knowing to allow for the validity of knowledge which is arrived at in a different way? For if God is God, then man can only come to know him in so far as God reveals himself to him, and in so far as man for his part allows himself to be drawn into relationship with the unknown. Here man will necessarily be receptive, obedient, listening, rather than giving, commanding, speaking. The prior activity must be God's. It would be misleading to say that man will necessarily be passive in this relationship. But he will be conscious that his acts do not originate in himself, but are drawn out and inspired by the acts of God. It is true that a way of approaching the Christian faith which makes its appeal to experience, and stresses the importance of entering into a shared tradition of insight and understanding, can have an attraction for a scientifically trained mind, in a way that other lines of approach cannot. But even so, to take the experiences of the saints and mystics seriously as sources of knowledge about God, and therefore also, in some sense, of illumination about the universe as a whole, is very difficult for us. It involves an uncomfortable enlarging of our perspectives; still more a readiness to accept data which fit awkwardly if at all into the framework of a naturalistic view of the universe.

But once we begin to recognise that the God who we believe has acted in a unique way, in Jesus, has never ceased to act in his world, then we shall begin to see that we cannot truly study the Gospel of Jesus in isolation but need to see it in relation to all that led up to it, and all that has followed from it. At its widest this must include the whole history of mankind. More immediately it means the history of the Old and New Israel. The things concerning Jesus cannot be understood without the illumination which comes both from the lives of the kings and prophets of the Old Testament, and from the lives of the saints of the Church. And here again the Eastern Orthodox tradition has something important to contribute, both in its extraordinary sense of a living continuity with the Fathers of the Church and the prophets of the Old Testament, so that in some sense they are felt to be contemporaries, and also in its awareness of the primacy of life and experience over systematic reflection and interpretation. We must not separate life from insight into life, history from interpretation. But it is true to say that it is the life and history of the Old Testament itself which form the primary preparation for the coming of the Christ, just as it is the living history of the Church, above all the lives of the saints, which provides the best commentary on the meaning of the Gospel.

The saints here are not of course regarded as outside the stream of common Christian experience and insight, but rather as points where that tradition has come most sharply and fully into focus. And here from the Reformation side we need to recognise the fact that there are those in whom the experience and knowledge, which in some degree are shared by all who believe, have developed and grown to an extent which we can scarcely imagine. There are those of whom we can only say that if there is a God they are taught by God, and who speak with a strange, self-authenticating authority, which is not unlike that of revelation itself. It is not for nothing that

Lossky gives so large a place towards the end of his book to an incident in the life of St Seraphim of Sarov. This nineteenth-century monk was not what the West would have called a 'trained theologian'. Rather he was a theologian in the earlier and fuller sense of the word, one who has drawn very close to the source from which theologising comes. Nor again is it by chance that one of the most remarkable pieces of Orthodox writing about God, man and the world in our own century, should be the work of a still more 'uneducated' monk, Staretz Silouan (*The Undistorted Image*, edited by Fr Sofrony). These are men who, if they speak of theology, do so because they have learnt of it from their own experience or, as they would say, from God, in their own experience. They are men who can say, as the New Testament writers say, *We know*, because what they know is the outcome of a lifetime's experience, not only a process of intellectual study. And this *We know* which is backed by a man's whole life, gains greater authority when it is evident that he who speaks it speaks not of himself alone, but as the mouthpiece of a whole community and a whole tradition.

Again we must guard against false disjunctions. The direct knowledge of the saint or the contemplative needs for its confirmation the subsequent reflection of the trained and systematic mind. It is the combination of St Anthony in the desert with St Athanasius in Alexandria which is so powerful in the fourth century. The tragedy is that in Western Christendom the two things should so often have fallen apart. But in our reflection on the meaning of the Christian tradition of belief in God, we must surely give a central place to the experience of the saints and contemplatives and recognise its creative value for the work of the systematic and reflective thinker. In any full consideration of this subject, we should need further to take into account the lives and utterances not only of Christian holy men, but also of those of other religious traditions. We should have to examine what in the 'mystical' tradition of mankind is common to all, what specific to various different ways. For if Christ is the one in whom all things hold together, then all striving after God must bear directly or indirectly upon the mystery revealed in him. But this would take us beyond the scope of this present book.

This direct and self-authenticating knowledge comes in many ways. It is by no means restricted to prayer in the narrow sense of the word. It comes through any act of obedience to God in service to the world, in service to our fellow-men. But there is one particular way in which it comes which deserves our attention here; a way which seems to have a particular significance for our own time, and a particular importance for the future of the debate about God. This is the way of contemplation as it is seen in the life of a contemplative community. In Protestantism, of course, such communities are only just beginning to appear. In Roman Catholicism the value of the contemplative element in monasticism was long over-shadowed by the stress laid upon the missionary and active usefulness of communities. But in Orthodoxy the primacy of the contemplative life within the monastic way, even in its final form in the life of the hermit, has been consistently seen for what it is, the ultimate form of the life of faith, in which man finds himself justified not by what he does, but by the grace and activity of God alone. This is not to say, of course, that such communities have any monopoly or exclusive right to this kind of knowledge of God. But it is to say that they provide a focal point for it, and a vivid witness to its present reality. In a world which is so deeply impressed by discursive and technological types of knowing, they are a sign of the possibility of another authentic and necessary form of human knowledge. This is a form of understanding, whose existence is fruitful for many different spheres of human life, and without which man cannot be fully man. It is linked with other types of insight, artistic, intuitive and symbolical, which all feel themselves menaced at the present time by a certain imbalance in the development of man's consciousness. Like all of them it contains a cognitive element which it is not easy for our age to recognise. But above all the existence of such communities is a living response to the question, does God have any existence apart from and beyond what we experience of him? For it is an existence which speaks by itself of the absolute dependence of man and the total transcendence of God, who is yet the one who comes down and establishes his dwelling at the centre of man's life and being.

To say this does not mean that either the Eastern Orthodox tradition or the contemplative communities as they are at present to be found both in Eastern and Western Christendom, can by themselves provide us with articulated answers to the questions raised in the current debate about God. It does mean that here are elements within the Christian tradition, too often overlooked or neglected, which have a vital part to play in the development of a living response to our current situation. As William Johnston remarks in a recent study of the growing dialogue between Christianity and the other world religions: 'One need be no great prophet to predict that Western theology of the next century will address itself primarily to dialogue with the great religions of the East. And I myself believe that this dialogue will be a miserable affair if the Western religions do not rethink their theology in the light of mystical experience.'[10] For Fr Johnston, writing from Tokyo, Greek and Russian Orthodoxy both belong to Western theology, and certainly any attempt to re-think the Christian tradition in the light of mystical experience, which did not start by placing the theology of the Greek Fathers in the centre of the picture, would be doomed to be a miserable affair. It is in the recovery of the wholeness and depth of our own tradition that we shall find how to enter most fruitfully into dialogue with others, just as it is that dialogue which stimulates us to go back and rediscover the treasure which lies hidden at the heart of our own inheritance.

NOTES

1. D. Jenkins. *Guide to the Debate about God*, 1966, p. 109
2. ibid., p. 42
3. ibid., p. 108
4. ibid., p. 42
5. ibid., p. 42
6. V. Lossky. *The Mystical Theology of the Eastern Church*, 1957, pp. 8–9
7. ibid., p. 39
8. op. cit., pp. 38–9
9. op. cit., p. 188
10. William Johnston, SJ. *The Inner Eye of Love, Mysticism and Religion*, 1978, pp. 9–10

The Fall of the 'God-Thing'
Reflections on Nathan Scott

One of the characteristics of our time in which questions of a theological kind have come to be reported by the mass media, is that we have been entertained by constant changes of theological fashion. In the 1960s we heard much about 'the death of God' and 'the theology of secularisation'; in the early 1970s we were alerted to a revival of enthusiastic, charismatic movements; more recently it has been the interest in the Eastern religions which has achieved the greatest notoriety. It would be foolish to pay too much attention to the details of such trends, which are in part created by our desire for sensation, and by the refusal of our society to take religious questions with full seriousness. But underneath them surely we can discern deeper and more abiding characteristics of our world; its painful sense of God's absence, his apparent unconcern, its sometimes frenzied and frustrated search for an awareness of the ultimate, the sacred.

Amongst those who have attempted to make sense of and to interpret these more permanent tendencies, is Nathan Scott, a scholar whose work is too little known on this side of the Atlantic, but who has established himself in the United States as a man who speaks with authority in many different areas, above all in contemporary literature on the one side, and in theology on the other. As one who has held chairs of theology and of English, a priest of the Episcopal Church as well as an academic, particularly perhaps as one who sees the world from inside a black and not a white skin, Nathan

Scott has a very particular contribution to make to our understanding of our times.

In 1966, at the time when interest in the work of the theologians of the death of God, Altizer, Hamilton and Van Buren, was at its height, Professor Scott published a book, *The Broken Center*, in which he made it plain that though he had much sympathy with their approach, he could not find it to be satisfying. It was not that he denied the significance and the weight of Nietzsche's proclamation of 'the death of God'; rather, as we shall see, he underlined it; nor that he felt inclined to conduct a rearguard action to defend conventionally accepted religious institutions and ideas. On the contrary his criticism of the then new theology was that it had accepted too readily the common criteria of meaning and relevance to be found in contemporary culture. He further argued that it had failed to notice that just as our world is full of evidence for the absence of God, so also it is not without indications of a search, however baffled, for the signs of his presence. By their enthusiastic, indeed ecstatic, acceptance of the thesis of the death of God, these writers had prejudged just those issues which theology ought always to keep open, and far from liberating man were in danger of enslaving him again.

. . . The new theology—in its servile attitude before the norms and standards of a positivistic culture—is close to expelling the Transcendent itself from our life-horizon. And it is just at this point that we can see something of the enormous price that a religionless Christianity is about to pay for the prize of 'relevance' in what is called a post-Christian world. For to say . . . that our world is furnished only with those realities that can be embraced by the scientific reason or by some form of quasi-scientific reason, to say that the range of our experience is limited to the public operables of empirical science and that we cannot even talk intelligibly about reality in any dimensions of ultimacy, is surely to confine the human spirit within an absolutely finite province of meaning. . . . And, in taking such a line as this, the new theology is not only in process of committing suicide, but, in choosing thus to co-operate with what is so profoundly dehumanizing in a radically profanized world, it is in effect helping to deepen the emptiness and the consequent despair which constitute the particular affliction of the men and women of our time. . . .[1]

Scott in no way denies the fact of this widespread and deep sense of a loss of meaning and direction in the experience of the twentieth century. His own knowledge of very varied areas of our culture prevents him from underestimating its significance.

However Nietzsche's message is finally to be assessed . . . we do unquestionably face today an immense body of testimony in philosophy and theology and imaginative literature of the last fifty years, whose purpose it is to suggest that behind the deep sense of loss in the twentieth century—of cultural order, even of what our psychologists call identity—is a sense of the loss of God.[2]

It simply will not do to try to minimise this great and shattering phenomenon, to say that it was all a misunderstanding. The 'God' who has died is not, we may believe, the true and living God of authentic Christian faith and experience, but he has certainly been a powerful figure in our Western European world, and one result of his disappearance seems to be that it is extremely difficult for our age to be aware of the presence of any other deity. The idol has effectively blocked the way of access to the reality which it hides. Some things, however, are becoming clear about this God who has died. Scott defines him, as do many others, as 'the God of traditional Western theism'. He is the all-powerful one, who keeps all things, and, above all, man, in subjection. Scott speaks of 'the notion of the *Deus ex machina,* of a supreme being to whose "existence" that of all other beings is subordinate'.[3] In *The Wild Prayer of Longing*, he speaks of

the conception of a supreme Being who, being eternally immutable and impassive, is forever unaffected by and consequently indifferent to all the endeavours and vicissitudes which make up the human story. For such a God, man's earthly pilgrimage is, ultimately, of no account, since nothing that we do or fail to do can augment or detract from the static perfection that this God enjoys.[4]

This is a God whose existence we think to demonstrate with rational proofs, the greatest being in the universe, an objectified Deity, 'the God-thing' as Scott describes him more than once. His transcendence is such that it needs to be jealously safeguarded. His impassibility must not be touched. But this we may feel is simply a caricature of any traditional Christian understanding of God. A caricature perhaps it is, but not without some likeness to an original. The temptation to prove God's existence, to control him, to manipulate him, to use him for our own ends, this has surely been strong in Western Christianity in recent centuries. We have reduced theology to a set of abstract formulae. One of the great spiritual directors of nineteenth-century French Catholicism, Abbé Huvelin, the spiritual father alike of Charles de Foucauld and Friedrich von Hügel, said of the theologians of his day, the springtime of neo-Scholasticism:

> As for me, I stick to realities; they, they have formulas. They do not perceive that life, all life, escapes analysis. What they dissect is a dead body. Something very small. Pass them by with a smile, a quiet smile. . . . Yes, I understand. What others would call proofs are only indications, hints, examples for you. Scholasticism, take St Thomas the greatest of the scholastics for instance, does not explain everything; the living truth escapes definition on every side. They think they can put the moon into a bottle; you could if it was a cheese.[5]

Both von Hügel and de Foucauld, in their very different ways, were men wholly present in the twentieth century and neither seems to have been conscious of the absence of God. Is it by chance that both had gained their vision of his presence in all things from a man so deeply conscious of the dangers of what has been called 'traditional theism'? Huvelin's remarks are a witness not only to the presence within the Churches of a tradition of understanding the things of God as mystery rather than problem, but also to the power of a philosophical and theological tradition which had done just the reverse, i.e. subjected the divine mystery to the exigencies of human logic.

Scott's method in face of this situation is not primarily to take up the question of theology itself, but rather to turn our attention to our own experience of living, as we find it expressed in the artistic works of our own and other times. Human existence itself, when deeply experienced and reflected on, bears witness to the presence of some transcendent element at its very heart.

> The human reality cannot legitimately be either thought or said to be merely an affair of surface and without depth . . . the deep things of self-knowledge and love, of suffering and joy and holiness, do always *withstand* exhaustive analysis, and thus offer a kind of attestation to the environing Mystery within which our lives are set.[6]

And, basing himself on the writings of Josef Pieper, he continues:

> The common, ordinary realities of our everyday existence suddenly open up and become transparent—and we are 'shaken': we are 'moved': and the world is disclosed as 'profounder, more all-embracing and mysterious than the logic of everyday reason has taught us to believe'. . . . So, in the kind of marvelling astonishment with which, in a given finite reality, we behold the fulness of Being, there is already implicit a certain sort of hope, and perhaps even of faith also. For, in the sense of wonder that our world elicits there is already a deep desire, a deep hope, that in the fulness of time we *shall* know fully, even if we do not now know fully: in other words, the essential structure of wonder . . . is the structure of hope and of faith.[7]

It is one of the functions of serious works of the imagination to re-awaken in us this sense of wonder at the meaning of the most ordinary things.

> For the strange greatness of the poet's task—of a Shakespeare, a Melville, a Tolstoi, an Eliot—involves his effort, through all the marvellous cunning of his craft, to arrange for another visitation being paid us by the concrete realities of our world (many of them long since familiar)—and one that will stir us into fresh apprehension of how really inexhaustible in fact they are. Is it not

the case, for example, that Shakespeare's Lear, Melville's Ahab, Tolstoi's Anna, and the dramatic actions of which they are a part testify, as it were, to the infinite depth and the radical mysteriousness of the human reality in the very disclosures that they bring to us of what is recalcitrantly finite in the world of the human creature?[8]

In the presence of such works as these we begin to be aware of our life in its dimension of depth, of inexhaustibility, of radical mystery. Here it is that we feel ourselves 'spoken' to by the deep things of ourselves and our world, as though they were but a taproot uniting the human reality with the ultimate Ground of all reality.[9]

From this discussion of the nature of our experience of human life in its mystery and finitude, Scott goes on to affirm:

It is, I believe, in some such way as this that poetic experience is suffused, in its intensest modes, with an awareness of the world, in its concrete phenomenality, as a sacrament of the divine immanence. And, of course, to be in the situation of beholding the world in its dimension of depth and to know ourselves searched and 'spoken' to by that depth is very nearly to be in the situation of prayer. . . .[10]

We discover that the word 'sacrament' here not only indicates the way in which a particular event or person or thing may suddenly become transparent to other and deeper realities. It also suggests that this moment of disclosure reveals a certain co-inherence of all things, some underlying unity of pattern. For the writer maintains that the 'esemplastic' or unifying power of the imagination is only a reflection of a unity already existing in things in themselves.

Though poetry addresses itself to the radically singular, concrete, individual aspects of reality, it has perennially been the wisdom of those who have reflected upon it most deeply (ever since Aristotle) to discern that, though it begins with the singular rather than the universal, it ends by somehow presenting both, by treating the singular in such a way that it becomes a glass of vision through which the universal may be seen. . . . The compelling power of 'things' to command the poet's attention flows from the relationships that the things exemplify and bespeak. . . . And, were it not for this inter-relationship amongst things, poetry would be impossible. Nothing that exists is an island unto itself; or, to change the metaphor, everything that holds membership in the world is an element of a seamless garment—the 'ragged edges' of every individual reality splay off into those of another, and 'the world is a wedding'. . . . (Poetry) wants to show how miraculously the concrete individual, when steadily contemplated, opens out into a kind of infinite depth and extension, so that its ultimate significance is discerned to flow from relations in which it stands to still other things consubstantial with itself.[11]

Such a way of looking at things is not, of course, the most customary in our society. This being willing to attend to things as they are, to let them speak to us, to reveal their own inner life and coherence, demands a quiet reflectiveness which we often do not find easy. Here not surprisingly we find in Nathan Scott a considerable influence from Heidegger's diagnosis of our present cultural and spiritual situation:

At the heart of our culture there is, Heidegger suggests, a profound perversion, a great imbalance that needs correction. At the end now of (as he nominates it) the History of Being in the West, what is lost is simply Being itself, and the great task awaiting the imagination is the recovery of a range of sympathy and conscience that will permit us to deal with the world in terms other than those simply of aggressive action. Our traditional habits of preference for what is assertive and bold and aggressive do indeed account for much that is distinctively a part of the impressive achievement of Western culture, but what Heidegger calls *the will to will* may also, as he sees, have the effect of so committing us to an essentially manipulative approach to reality that all attentiveness to the sheer ontological weight and depth of the world is lost. And this is precisely the sort of loss that he believes to threaten in such an advanced technological culture as our own, where our great temptation is to be so bent upon bringing the

world to heel, that we risk its becoming totally devoured by the
engines of our science and ideology.[12]

We have to learn not to deal with the world 'solely in terms of
mastery and control and manipulation', to free ourselves from the
'essentially predatory motive that constitutes the sovereign passion
dominating the mentality of our period'.[13]

If we could once be free to attend to the universe in a way totally
different from this, we might find that we should discover things
not only about the world itself, but about the world 'as a sacrament
of the divine immanence'. It is this thought which becomes predominant in Scott's book, *The Wild Prayer of Longing*, since he feels
that it is this search that is becoming increasingly evident in our
time.

> One feels [he writes in the introduction] wherever one turns in
> this strange, late time, that, beneath the flamboyance and anti-
> nomianism which are everywhere rampant, the prompting pas-
> sion by which men are today coming more and more to be most
> deeply moved is a great need—in the absence of God—to find the
> world in which we dwell to be, nevertheless, in some sort truly a
> sacramental economy. . .[14]

But surely if this is to be possible, it will be necessary to say
something more about the divine, than simply to acknowledge the
death of 'the God of Western theism'. Scott recognises that this is
so, and speaks in this book of 'a line of speculation reaching from
Ruysbroeck through Angelus Silesius to Paul Tillich and from Eckhart and Boehme to Nicolas Berdyaev'. It is, he suggests, a line of
thought which does not deny

> the conception of reality as ultimately personal, as ultimately
> possessing the same kind of steadiness belonging to personal
> relationships characterised by mutuality of trust and love. Yet it
> is a tradition which distrusts the anthropomorphic image as a
> vehicle for the expression of the personalist vision. . . .[15]

Here, too, he finds the possibility of another and more flexible understanding of the divine transcendence, in which we could, maybe, conceive of God as transcending his transcendence in order to establish himself at the heart of the world which he has created.

Nathan Scott speaks with considerable respect of this 'minority tradition in Western religious and philosophical thought', which, granted all the variety of thinkers included in it, he designates under the title 'panentheist', and he recognises its place in the background of Heidegger's work. Still, he seems to say, it is only a minority tradition. And it is just at this point that one would wish to ask whether he and nearly all of those involved in this discussion have taken sufficiently into account another element in the history of Christian experience and reflection, the Eastern Orthodox? If, for instance, we go back to Ruysbroeck, do we not find him rooted in this earlier tradition? Is it not here that there is the vital clue to unravelling the tangle of our Western situation, the way towards a vision of the God who is truly the living God of Christian faith and experience, not the majestic monolith of a powerful but limited philosophical theology? Certainly in Eastern Orthodoxy there has never been that divorce between mysticism and theology which has had such an unfortunate effect in the West since the thirteenth century. The names whom one might cite in favour of a very different understanding of God's relation to the world from that attributed to Western theism are central and authoritative in the whole Eastern tradition, theological and spiritual alike, a Gregory of Nyssa, a Maximus the Confessor, a John of Damascus, a Gregory Palamas. Let us for a moment see what they would have to say in face of the situation, as Nathan Scott has outlined it.

First there is the question of God as *a* being, even the greatest, *an* object, even an omnipotent one. We may take St John of Damascus as one of the most systematic and influential of Eastern thinkers.

> God does not belong to the class of existing things: not that he has no existence, but that he is above all existing things, nay even above existence itself. For if all forms of knowledge have to do with that which exists, assuredly that which is above knowledge must certainly be also above essence; and conversely that which is above essence will also be above knowledge.[16]

Of course, as Lossky points out, to say that God in himself is wholly beyond our knowledge is not, in Eastern Orthodoxy, to fall into some kind of agnosticism, nor is it to indulge in 'a theology of ecstasy'. It is precisely the way in which the knowledge of God is safeguarded from the manipulative tendencies of the human intellect, which seeks proofs and guarantees.

But if God in his own being is unknowable in Eastern theology, nonetheless he makes himself known *in his energies,* which are truly God himself present and at work in the world. Orthodoxy carefully and constantly avoids all tendencies to pantheism, maintaining the distinction between creator and creature, and affirming that, even in being restored to unity in God, the multiplicity of creation is not lost but preserved. At the same time it has a view of the relation of God to the world in which God is seen as most intimately involved with his creation through the uncreated energies.

> That which western theology calls by the name of the *supernatural* signifies for the East the *uncreated.* . . . The difference consists in the fact that the western conception of grace implies the idea of causality, grace being represented as an effect of the divine Cause . . . while for eastern theology, there is a natural procession, the energies, shining forth eternally from the divine essence.[17]
>
> Eastern theology . . . refuses to ascribe to the divine nature the character of an essence locked within itself. God . . . is more than essence: he overflows his essence, manifests himself beyond it, and being incommunicable by nature, communicates himself.[18]

God transcends his own transcendence.

This God who is present throughout the world in his creative energies has made man in his image and likeness and placed him at the heart of things. Here again the intimacy and reciprocity of God's relationship with man is conceived more strongly in Eastern Orthodoxy than in the West. The Eastern Fathers do not hesitate to say that God became man in order that man might become God. Summing up the teaching of Maximus the Confessor, Thunberg says: 'Deification is as it were simply the other side of Incarnation— i.e. incarnation both in Jesus and in the individual—and thus it takes place wherever this incarnation takes place. . . .'[19] And Maximus himself says, 'The Word of God, who is God, wills always and in all things to work the mystery of his incarnation.'

In such a vision of things there will be room neither for an anti-humanist religion, nor for an anti-religious humanism. God is not against man but for him, not above man but beside him; and if always beyond man, yet at the same time at the heart of his journey. The whole world is seen as sacramental of the divine presence, full of God's glory. It is notorious that Eastern Christianity has developed a fuller reflection on the nature of images than the West, and that its vision of God's redemptive action always includes the whole creation.

> When that which is transcendent of every particular being, yet present in every being as the power whereby it is enabled to be—when this *Mysterium Tremendum* is declared to be holy, then the world is by way of being envisaged as a truly sacramental universe, as an outward and visible expression of an inward and spiritual grace.[20]

This time the quotation is not from an Eastern writer but from Nathan Scott, summing up his own interpretation of Heidegger.

This apparently unexpected juxtaposition of Heidegger and Maximus may suggest that the vision of the nature of things which Nathan Scott is outlining is not so absent from Christian tradition as many people are inclined to think. It is a vision which has very much in common with the tradition of one half of the Christian world, and the half which, though its witness is little heeded in the West, yet has a right to claim that it has faithfully preserved the inner experience and understanding of the first Christian centuries. The death of 'the God of Western theism', the destruction of the idol, is opening the way to a rediscovery of the acts of the God of Abraham, of Isaac and of Jacob, the living God of the worship and confession of the Fathers of the Church, he who makes himself fully known in Jesus Christ, and wno in his Word and his Spirit is present and at work throughout the whole of what he has made.

NOTES

1. B. pp. 173–4. In this chapter Nathan Scott's books will be identified as follows: B = *The Broken Centre*, 1966. N = *Negative Capability*, 1969. W = *The Wild Prayer of Longing*, 1971
2. B. p. 147
3. B. p. 149
4. W. p. 54
5. From advice given to Friedrich von Hügel in May 1886. *Selected Letters of Friedrich von Hügel*, pp. 58 and 61
6. B. p. 174
7. B. pp. 175–6
8. N. pp. 101–2
9. N. p. 101
10. N. p. 103
11. N. pp. 99ff
12. N. p. 66
13. W. p. 66
14. W. p. xiv
15. W. pp. 56–7
16. Quoted in V. Lossky, *The Mystical Theology of the Eastern Church*, p. 36
17. ibid., p. 88
18. ibid., p. 240
19. Lars Thunberg. *Microcosm and Mediator*, pp. 458–9
20. W. p. 73

II

THE LIFE-GIVING SPIRIT

Symeon, the New Theologian: the Singer of Fire and Light

I

One of the many unexpected changes which have occurred in the Christian world during the last twenty-five years relates to the question of 'speaking in tongues'. Twenty-five years ago the subject of glossolalia seemed rather remote, a topic to be discussed perhaps in a study of I Corinthians, but hardly a matter of practical concern. Now if we have not received the gift of tongues ourselves it is quite likely that we shall have Christian friends who have done so. In a quarter of a century a movement of prayer and spiritual renewal has effected all the Churches, and this particular phenomenon which is a secondary, though sometimes spectacular, aspect of it has come to be very widely known. It is a movement which has taken no notice of denominational boundaries. In the last ten years its influence seems to have been strongest in the Roman Catholic Church where it has claimed the support of leaders of the stature of Cardinal Suenens, and academic theologians of the calibre of Heribert Mühlen, author of two classical works in German on the doctrine of the Holy Spirit. 'I would like simply to say', he is reported to have said, 'that for fifteen years I have known the Holy Spirit with my head, but now I also know him with my heart and I wish the same joy to you.'[1] Thus a movement which had its origins in the holiness element in Methodism has come to spread its influence throughout the Christian world.

One of the unexpected results of this development has been to make us look again at forgotten corners of Church history. The Jesuits for instance find in the diary of their founder, St Ignatius of Loyola, that at a certain moment in his life he received both the gift of tears and the gift of tongues. Some of the more startling incidents in the ministry of John Wesley sound less remote, when colleagues tell us of people falling down in a kind of trance, being 'slain in the Spirit'. Enthusiasm has certainly not died. Indeed at a time when new sects and new religions abound, it is especially important for the Churches to discover how to let the element of enthusiastic and fervent devotion grow and flourish within the Christian fellowship. It becomes imperative to understand how such movements may be contained within the tradition, bringing it new vitality, and how the non-rational elements of religion may be saved from becoming anti-rational and simply sliding away into the sands of sectarianism.

II

At the beginning of his classical introduction to the history of Methodism, Rupert Davies discerns seven characteristics which he believes to be typical of movements of a Methodist kind, wherever they occur in Church history, and all of which, to some degree or other, seem to me to occur in the current movements of renewal. They are briefly: (1) a whole-hearted acceptance of traditional Christian doctrine coupled with the conviction that such doctrine is useless unless verified in life and experience, (2) a strong emphasis on the personal relationship of the believer with Jesus Christ as Lord and Saviour, (3) an equally strong emphasis on the work of the Holy Spirit, (4) a serious attempt to embody life in Christ in actual groups and communities of committed men and women, (5) a desire for the proclamation of the Gospel to all mankind, (6) a concern for the material well-being as well as the spiritual needs of the poor, (7) a tendency to bring together lay people and the ordained in new structures of shared life and ministry.[2]

It is not my purpose in this chapter to see how far these seven marks could be found to characterise the charismatic movement, though in fact I think we could find clear traces of all or nearly all of them in its typical representatives. Rather I want to turn to another moment in Church history, and to the life of a particular individual to see what light it can shed on the way in which movements of enthusiastic devotion may be integrated into the Christian tradition as a whole. If I have a disagreement with Mr Davies it is not at all over his way of describing such movements, but rather over the places in Church history where he looks for their most striking examples. In this chapter I want to look to the Christian East and examine one of the greatest figures in the spiritual tradition of Orthodoxy, St Symeon, the New Theologian.

The fact that Symeon's name is scarcely known in the West, tells us more about the gulf between Christian East and West than it does about Symeon, as Dr Anna-Marie Aagaard, a Danish scholar, herself a theologian of the Holy Spirit, remarks.[3] Symeon without question is one of the great figures of the Eastern Orthodox tradition, and I would dare to say one of the greatest of all Christian mystics. There are indeed remarkable similarities between some aspects of his teaching and that of John and Charles Wesley. There is a strange similarity between the situation in which he lived and the response he made to it, and the situation of the Wesleys.

Symeon was born in Paphlagonia in Asia Minor in the year 949. He came from an aristocratic family and as a young man he held a minor position in the Imperial court. His first deep experience of Christ came to him when he was living in the world. Only in 977 did he enter upon the way of the monastic life, a way which he followed through various vicissitudes till the time of his death in 1022.

The first thing that we need to notice about him is the title which he has acquired in Orthodox tradition; Symeon, the New Theologian. There are only three men to whom the title 'Theologian' is given: the first is St John, the Apostle and the Evangelist, St John the Divine; the second is St Gregory Nazianzen the most poetical of the group of great Christian thinkers in the fourth century who did so much to articulate the doctrine of the Trinity. The third is our Symeon. To understand the use of the word 'Theologian' here, we need to remember the inseparable link between prayer and theology in Eastern tradition. Theology is the direct intuitive knowledge of God. The Eastern Church reserves this title for its great visionaries, for those who can gaze into the mystery of God's being and God's love, and then express their vision in poetic prayer and praise. In the more recent history of the Christian West we might perhaps think of St John of the Cross and Charles Wesley as prime candidates for this title of Theologian.

But Symeon is the *New* Theologian. He occurs at a time when men were hardly looking for such a phenomenon, when the Eastern Christian Empire and the Eastern Christian Church had become set in their ways, somewhat rigid in the splendour of their institutions. It is into such an atmosphere that Symeon bursts with his insistence that the life and experience of the Christian now is no different from that of the first apostles. Everything that was given to them is in principle given to us. For him it is the quintessence of all heresies to say that it is impossible that men now should be able to experience and know the depth of faith that the apostles knew, should be without the spiritual powers and gifts with which they were endowed.

The good news of God's forgiveness in Jesus Christ strikes him with all the force of its unbelievable newness.

> What is this new marvel which is happening now again?
> Now again God wills to appear to sinners. . .
> What is this manifestation of goodness to man which has just appeared,
> Strange out-pouring of gentleness, new source of mercy . . .?[4]

We have come already to the first of the characteristics of Methodism. It accepts the tradition of Christian faith whole-heartedly, but it believes that that faith must be known and experienced personally in life and devotion. This is one of the most striking points of the teaching of Symeon and one of the points where at least in emphasis he differs from much of the tradition of Eastern Orthodoxy. It is common enough in that tradition, as in other Christian communions, to say that God's grace usually works in us without our being consciously aware of it. The sacraments are effective without our having any immediate feeling of them. Grace acts at a level below that of consciousness and feeling. This is certainly the point of view most commonly held in my own Church, and I recognise much good sense in it. Its danger is to be found when it reaches the point of saying that we ought never to expect this consciousness and feeling of God's action within us and when it thus discourages people from expecting any direct awareness of God. St Symeon, however, will have none of all this. Again and again he insists that we must feel and know the power of God at work in our conversion. It is not enough that we have received the Holy Spirit. We must be consciously aware of it. The intransigence of this teaching in St Symeon can sometimes trouble Orthodox believers. They do not seem to have this kind of experience.

It is scarcely necessary to point out how close this insistence is to the teaching of the Wesleys. I take two verses almost at random from the hymns for the Lord's Supper.

Nay, but this is his will
(We know it and feel),
That *we* should partake
The banquet for all he so freely did make.

In rapturous bliss,
He bids us do this,
The joy it imparts
Hath witnessed his gracious design in our hearts.[5]

Notice that knowing goes together with feeling. The experience being spoken of in Symeon and the Wesleys is not purely emotional. It is cognitive as well.

From this insistence on the conscious awareness of God's work within us, there follows very naturally the second of the points enumerated by Rupert Davies, the sense of a personal relationship with Jesus as Saviour. As John Meyendorff remarks in his study *Byzantine Theology*, 'Symeon stands for the basic understanding of Christianity as personal communion with, and vision of God.'[6] But we may let Symeon speak for himself. Like Charles Wesley he is at a stand to know where to begin.

How shall I describe, Master, the vision of your countenance?
How should I speak of the unspeakable contemplation of your
    beauty?

How can the sound of my words contain him whom the world
   cannot contain?
How can anyone express your love for mankind?

And he goes on to speak in a very personal fashion of an experience
of Christ which had come to him. He describes this inner experience
with a detail which is unusual in the Eastern tradition, where in
general there is greater reticence in speaking of what is most intimate and inward.

For I was seated in the light of a lamp that was shining on me.
And it was illuminating the darkness and the shadows of night.
It seemed indeed to me that in the light I was occupied in
   reading.
As if I were scrutinising the words and examining the proposi-
   tions.

Here, we may interject, is an image of the Christian studying the
Bible, reflecting on Christian doctrine in the light of the lamp of the
meditating mind. And then something happens. There is a direct
intervention from above.

Then as I was meditating, Master, on these things,
Suddenly you appeared from above, much greater than the sun,
And you shone brilliantly from the heavens down into my
   heart. . . .
At once I forgot the light of the lamp
I didn't remember that I was inside the house. . . .
Moreover I forgot my body completely.
I said to you and now I say it from the depths of my heart:
Have mercy on me, Master, have mercy on me
Who have never truly served you at all, O Saviour. . . .
I had my share in every kind of sin of soul and body. . . .
Therefore it is towards me that you most demonstrate your
   mercy,
Towards me who have sinned so exceedingly more than others.
It was you yourself who said that it was not the healthy who have
   need of a physician, but the sick.

As my sickness is so great, as I have been so negligent,
So pour out your great pity on me, O Word.
But O what intoxication of light, what movement of fire,
O what swirling of flame within me, wretch that I am,
Coming from you and your glory.
This glory I know and I say it, it is your Holy Spirit. . . .[7]

This description of the coming of the heavenly fire calls to mind
one of the greatest of Pantycelyn's verses.

It is a flame of fire from midmost heaven
that came down hither into the world,
fire that will kindle my stubborn nature,
fire that will fill the breadth of my mind:
it will not fail
while God remains in being.

Often Symeon speaks of tears, tears alike of joy and repentance, in
this moment of divine encounter. One is reminded of Ernest Rattenbury's words in his study of Charles Wesley's hymns: 'It may still
be questioned whether any lenses have yet been constructed as perfect for visualising Jesus as penitent tears. Charles Wesley shed
many, which, though they dimmed his sight, clarified his vision.'[8]
Sometimes this meeting with Christ is described in terms of a first
vision of light in which Symeon had felt himself to be pulled up out
of the mud and slime of a sinful life. At other times he reflects on the
mystery of our incorporation into Christ, and this particularly in his
prayers of thanksgiving after Holy Communion.

You make your home in each one of us and you live in everyone
And for all of us you become our home and we live in you. . . .
We become members of Christ and Christ becomes our
    members,
Christ becomes my hand, Christ my foot,
And I, wretch that I am, I am become Christ's hand,
    Christ's foot. . . .[9]

It is important to note that this very personal sense of communion

with Christ has its roots in the Eucharist. The conviction about our
bodily relationship with Christ is particularly strong in Symeon. His
whole vision of spiritual life is very much in flesh and blood. In this
sense he is very close to St Paul. He seems also to have owed much to
the example of his spiritual father, Symeon the Pious, a monk of
Stoudion, who he tells us had no shame of nakedness but quite
simply was able to regard his own body and the bodies of others as
temples of the Holy Spirit.

For if, as we have said, Symeon's devotion is marked by this
awareness of personal relationship with Christ, still more is it
marked by a conviction about the power and presence of the Holy
Spirit. In fact, Symeon might without exaggeration be called the
theologian, the singer of the Spirit. For him it is the Spirit who is at
work in all things in the Christian life.

> Do not say that it is impossible to receive the Divine Spirit.
> Do not say that without him you can be saved.
> Do not say that one can possess him without knowing it.
> Do not say that God cannot be seen by men.
> Do not say that men do not see the divine light
> Or that this is impossible in these present times.[10]

The Spirit comes to us from God, teaching us by a way other than
that of men, overthrowing our human wisdom and our human cer-
tainties.

> The Spirit has been sent by the Son to men
> Not to the unbelieving, nor to the friends of fame,
> Not to the rhetoricians, or philosophers,
> Not to those who have studied the works of the Greeks,
> Not to those who do not know the Scriptures,
> Not to those who play a role on the world's stage,
> Not to those who speak affectedly and with many words. . . .
> But to those who are poor in spirit and in life,
> To those who are pure of heart and body,
> To those who speak simply, live more simply
> And whose thinking is simpler still,
> Who shun renown like the fire of hell

And hate flatteries from the bottom of their heart. . . .[11]

One of the most moving elements in Symeon's teaching about the Holy Spirit is to be found in his insistence that in the Spirit God adapts himself to the condition of each one, comes down to be with man at the lowest place of his need.

When man is filled with remorse and weeps
He, the Spirit, is called water, for he cleanses.
He unites with man's tears and washes away all stain.
When with his help affliction cools the anger of the heart
Then he takes the name of gentleness.
When, thanks to him, man blazes up against unrighteousness
Then he takes the name of zeal.
Again he is called peace and joy and goodness
Because to him who grieves he grants the one and the other
And makes joy break forth in the heart like a spring.
From this spring pour forth compassion and mercy
To all men, but above all to those who wish to turn and be saved.
For he has mercy on all, but he works together with those
Who turn to him, he helps them and encourages them
And shares their sufferings. . . .[12]

There is much more that could be said about St Symeon's teaching on the Holy Spirit. It needs of course to be seen against the background of the whole Eastern Christian tradition in which the role of the Holy Spirit in prayer and worship, in the sacrament of the Eucharist, for instance, is more explicitly affirmed than it has been in the West. But let it suffice to cite some words of Fr Kallistos Ware on this subject of a personal participation in the Holy Spirit.

What emerges unmistakably from St Symeon's *Discourse* is the crucial importance which he attached to personal experience, to an immediate awareness of the Holy Spirit with full consciousness and 'in perception of soul'. He believed that, alike in the ministry of spiritual direction and in every aspect of the Christian life, the one thing necessary is a direct and conscious knowledge of the working of the Paraclete. All formalism, any suggestion that

grace can be transmitted *ex opere operato* or that a man can be a
Christian at second hand, he most vehemently repudiated. . . . If
a man is to be within the Tradition, much more is demanded of
him than a verbal conformity to doctrinal standards and a correct
participation in liturgical rites. He must know God the Holy
Spirit in 'perception of soul'.[13]

III

The fourth characteristic of a Methodist type of movement according
to our original description is that it should seek 'to embody the "life
in Christ" of which the New Testament speaks, in personal and
social "holiness", and in the formation for this purpose of small
groups of committed people who will encourage, correct, instruct,
edify and support each other.' In so far as a large part of Symeon's life
was spent in building up and reforming monastic communities, we
may say that here again he fits into the picture. For the description
of the small committed group, though it was not, I suppose, primarily intended to refer to monastic communities, in fact suits them
very well. As we may imagine, Symeon was a man who demanded
much of the monks under his charge. This was at times a cause of
opposition in his life.

Fifthly, there comes 'the desire to make known the Gospel, and
above everything else the love and pity of God, for each individual
sinner, on the widest possible scale and in the most persuasive
possible terms'. Here of course there is no comparison between
Symeon as abbot and writer, and John Wesley as travelling preacher
and evangelist. And yet even here there is some similarity. The
purpose of Symeon's writing is to cry aloud to all men the wonders of
the unmerited grace that he has found, to call men to share in God's
gift. He compares himself to a beggar who, having received a piece
of gold, runs to show his companions what he has been given. At the
end of one of his works he declares: 'And then we speak to all our
brethren. Fathers, brothers, monks, you who live in the world, rich
and poor, slaves and freemen, young and old, men of all ages and all

races, hear.'[14] And he goes on to address emperors and patriarchs, in a tone of prophetic authority and urgency. It is true that his teaching emerges from a monastic milieu and is often addressed in the first instance to monks. But it is not restricted to them. In his own time and ever since it has been heard and attended to by multitudes of men and women living in the world.

The sixth characteristic relates to the desire to relieve material poverty as well as spiritual need. Here again I do not know of any particular philanthropic schemes promoted by St Symeon. But there can be no doubt of his concern for the poor. He bases the duty of alms-giving on the strongest possible foundation; the words of the Lord 'in so much as you did it to the least of these my brethren you did it to me.' He writes:

> If Christ has deigned to take on the visage of every poor man and has made himself like every poor man, it was with this purpose: that none of those who believe should raise himself above his brother, but that each one, considering his brother and his neighbour as his God, should count himself lower not in relation to his brother, but in relation to God, who has made him, and thus welcome and honour him, and spend his resources in his service, just as Christ our God poured out his blood for our salvation.[15]

The discovery of God present within us, of God present in the sacrament of the Eucharist is joined with the discovery of God present in the poor and dispossessed. As St John Chrysostom says, we shall not find Christ at the altar in Church, unless we are also finding him in the homeless outside.

The final mark of a movement of a Methodist type concerns the collaboration of lay and ordained in the whole range of Christian ministry. Here again, in the very different circumstances of the life of St Symeon the New Theologian, we can find a kind of parallel. In one who emphasises so strongly the need for inner experience and is so scornful of any merely formal religion, we might expect to find a tendency to devalue the Church's institutional hierarchy, in favour of the hierarchy of holiness. And this is indeed precisely what we do find. No other writer of the Eastern Orthodox tradition comes so near to saying that the spiritual reality of the ministry is taken away from those who, though duly ordained, have not lived in a way worthy of their calling. This point Symeon makes with particular sharpness in relation to the ministry of spiritual fatherhood and the remission of sins. This was to him a particularly urgent matter. In his own life the role of his spiritual father, Symeon the Pious, had been of crucial significance. But the older Symeon was a lay monk and not a priest. The practice of making one's confession to a lay monk who is a man of genuine spiritual discernment has been known through the centuries in Eastern Orthodoxy and is still known to this day. But few have stressed its importance over against the ministry of the sacramental hierarchy in the way in which Symeon did.

We might well ask how it was possible that such a man could be held within the structures of a strictly hierarchical Church. It was not done without difficulty. Symeon became involved in controversy over these very topics, and in 1009 was sentenced to exile from which he chose not to return. The enthusiastic tone of his writing, his stress on the necessity for personal experience of the action of the Holy Spirit were certainly not universally welcomed during his lifetime. Nevertheless Symeon was soon recognised as a saint, and though some of his opinions may not have been accepted in the Orthodox Church, in general the influence of his writings has been immense. In this recognition of his life and teaching Meyendorff sees a sign that for Eastern Orthodoxy, 'the Spirit alone is the ultimate criterion of truth and the only final authority.'[16]

We must, I believe, also see here an example of the way in which the Eastern Christian tradition has managed to maintain a reciprocity and a balance between different elements in the Church, which have too often become separated in the West. In his study of Orthodox doctrine, *The Mystical Theology of the Eastern Church*, Vladimir Lossky insists that there are two aspects of the Church. It is first the Body of Christ, the historically founded institution with its continuous sacramental life and ministry representing the givenness of the divine revelation. The Church is also the communion of the Holy Spirit, a body marked by personal freedom and initiative, by the ever new and constantly unexpected activity of the Spirit. Both the element of institution and the element of event are necessary to the Church. There is a succession of the saints, men and women of personal insight and holiness, which complements and fulfils the external succession of doctrinal teaching and sacramental ministry. Symeon himself speaks of this succession of the saints from generation to generation as forming a kind of 'golden chain' which is not easily broken.[17]

Precisely how these two aspects of the Church are held together in one, may not be easy to explain. Meyendorff speaks of the way in which, in the Orthodox vision of things: 'the Spirit simultaneously guarantees the continuity and authenticity of the Church's sacramental institutions and bestows upon each human person a possibility of free divine experience, and, therefore, a full responsibility for both personal salvation and corporate continuity of the Church in the divine truth.'[18] Certainly there is a remarkable combination of what is corporate and what is personal, of freedom and authority, in the Eastern church, symbolised in the important role of the lay theological scholars. No less certainly there is a striking combination of personal experience with sacramental structure. At the very centre of the Eucharist, when it is celebrated according to the Liturgy of St John Chrysostom, just before the moment of communion the priest pours hot water into the chalice, with the words, 'The fervour of faith, full of the Holy Spirit.' Whatever the historical origin of this gesture may have been, in its present form it speaks eloquently of the presence of pentecostal fire, personal fervour at the heart of the Church's worship.

Behind this concern to maintain the two aspects of the Church together, there lie, I believe, two things. First there is a resolutely Biblical emphasis on the unity of man, body, soul and spirit. Life in the Spirit is not disembodied. It involves the whole of ourselves turned towards God. The Spirit is active in the material world, in the body of man in the body of the Church, both of which become his dwelling place. Secondly, and very closely linked with this, is a sense of the priority of the personal. The Church is not a suprapersonal collective but a communion of free persons, an image in the created world of the Tri-personal life of God himself. Everything in the Church exists for the building up of persons in love, and the life of each person demands the element of spontaneity and growth as well as of stability and order. All this is not something abstract or theoretical. It is given and received in personal relationships, working itself out in flesh and blood. The theologian is one who bears witness to what he has heard and seen of the transforming action of God in the flesh and blood of human history. As Rattenbury says of Charles Wesley: 'His theology is an account of truth realised in personal experiment and experience ... his soul and mind were supplied, not from cisterns, but from springs; his teaching was not merely of a school but of a genuine experience of life—the divine life.'[19]

So it is for St Symeon that the theologian is not one who has simply learnt from books; still less is he one who constructs an abstract conceptual system. For Symeon, as for Charles Wesley, it is in life through penitence and adoration that the way opens up into the knowledge of God. His teaching follows on in a tradition which goes back into the Scriptures through the first centuries of the Greek and Semitic-speaking Churches. It points the way forward to the developed teaching of St Gregory Palamas in the fourteenth century, when this theology of insight and experience comes into head-on collision with a theology of intellectual speculation much influenced by the scholasticism of the West. Of course, in these Orthodox writers the appeal to experience is not used as a substitute for the appeal to the authority of Scripture and Tradition; they are presupposed. As Lossky says: 'Outside the truth kept by the whole Church personal experience would be deprived of all certainty, all objectivity. It would be a mingling of truth and falsehood, of reality and of illusion: "mysticism" in the bad sense of the word.' But without the element of personal appropriation, all would remain coldly formal and external. 'The teaching of the Church would have no hold on souls if it did not in some degree express an interior experience of truth, granted in different measure to each one of the faithful.'[20] The great theologians, in this sense, are those who have received in overflowing measure this gift which is common to all who believe. They are those who can say with the apostolic writer: 'That which was from the beginning, which we have heard, which we have seen with our eyes, which we have looked upon, and our hands have handled, of the Word of life ... that which we have seen and heard declare we unto you.'[21]

It is this conviction that stands at the heart of the work of a theologian like Lossky. This from the Orthodox view-point is still the true nature of theology. 'For Christianity is not a philosophical school for speculating about abstract concepts, but it is essentially a communion with the living God.'[22] This is why the Orthodox approach to theology 'utterly excludes all abstract and purely intellectual theology which would adapt the mysteries of God to human ways of thought. It is an existential attitude which involves the whole man; there is no theology apart from experience; it is necessary to change, to become a new man. No one who does not follow the path of union with God can be a theologian.'[23] It is highly significant that the penultimate chapter of Lossky's book should be full of quotations from the writings of St Symeon, and that it also contains an account of the famous conversation between the nineteenth-century Russian saint, Seraphim of Sarov, and his disciple Nicholas Motovilov. In the course of that conversation the master defines the aim of Christian life to be the acquisition of the Holy Spirit, and the disciple sees the old man transfigured by the divine light. We are here very far from any anti-intellectual obscurantism, as the slightest acquaintance with Orthodox writing will show. What we are meeting is a level of biblical realism, which looks for a transformation of man's mind, as well as of his heart, and which recognises clearly the limitations in divine matters of the unconverted intellect.

IV

At the beginning of this essay, I suggested that the tradition of the Christian East might be able to throw some light on the great movement of the Spirit which took place in England in the eighteenth century, and also on the widespread movements of our own time in which, despite all the ambiguities of human life, we think to discern the action of the Spirit today. In remembering the work of John and Charles Wesley, our attitude must rightly be one of thankfulness for all that God has done through their ministry. But for an Anglican there cannot help being also a strain of sadness and repentence, when he thinks of the failure of the Church of England as a whole to respond to what God was doing through them, a failure of response which in the end led to a schism which greatly impoverished those on both sides of it. And when we come to our own day no one who is in contact with the charismatic movement can be unaware of the dangers of divisiveness which are present within it, particularly when it gets cut off from the main body of the Church and falls prey to a narrow-minded and anti-intellectual theology. If the Church has need of the new enthusiasts, they, too, have need of the wisdom of the Christian centuries. We need wisdom and discernment not only to heal the breaches of the past but also to avoid the creation of new schisms in the future. Anything which can help us to see how to hold together institution and event, Word and Spirit, is surely to be welcomed.

But in conclusion I would want to make a more extreme and paradoxical suggestion. What is necessary is not so much that we should take one or two hints from the East to solve our Western problems, adding a touch of exotic, Oriental colour to the familiar pattern of our Western Christianity. No, the requirement is greater than that. It is that we should be willing to let our whole way of posing the questions, our whole set of pre-suppositions be challenged by the radically different nature of the Eastern tradition. We should seek to place our questions in a new context, and let our perspectives be correspondingly transformed by a direct encounter with the reality of Orthodoxy. For here is another way of living, thinking and praying the mystery of the one Gospel of Christ, a way which, for all its own limitations, has managed to hold together freedom and authority, clerical and lay, personal experience and corporate life in a pattern which seems to correspond to the complex nature of man, himself created in the image of the Triune God. This is a pattern which is grounded in the faith that the divine grace is always at work, healing what is wounded and making up what is lacking in the creation, that the Holy Spirit is everywhere present and filling all things and that only in his presence can we rise up into the calling which God has given to us, to become his free children.

This is an enlarged version of a lecture originally given in Wesley's Chapel in Bristol on 24 May 1978.

NOTES

1. René Laurentin. *Catholic Pentecostalism*, 1977, p. 185
2. Rupert Davies. *Methodism*, 1963, pp 11–12
3. Anna-Marie Aagaard. *Tema og Tolkninger*, 1976, p. 86
4. St Symeon, the New Theologian. *Hymns of Divine Love* (translated by G. A. Maloney, SJ), n.d., p. 36
5. H. A. Hodges and A. M. Allchin (eds). *A Rapture of Praise*, 1966, p. 147
6. John Meyendorff. *Byzantine Theology*, 1974, p. 74
7. Maloney. op. cit., p. 135
8. J. Ernest Rattenbury. *The Evangelical Doctrines of Charles Wesley's Hymns*, 1941, p. 158
9. Maloney. op. cit., p. 54
10. Maloney. op. cit., p. 145
11. Maloney. op. cit., p. 96
12. Maloney. op. cit., p. 111
13. K. T. Ware. 'Tradition and Personal Experience in Later Byzantine Theology' in *Eastern Churches Review* Vol III, No. 2, Autumn 1970, pp. 137–9
14. Symeon, Le Nouveau Théologien. *Traites Théologiques et Ethiques* (Sources Chrétiennes 122), 1966, Vol. I, p. 431
15. Symeon, Le Nouveau Théologien. *Chapitres Théologiques, Gnostiques et Pratiques* (Sources Chrétiennes 51), 1957, p. 111
16. John Meyendorff. op. cit., p. 75
17. *Chapitres Théologiques* . . . p. 81
18. John Meyendorff. op. cit., p. 177
19. Rattenbury. op. cit., pp., 85, 87
20. Vladimir Lossky. *The Mystical Theology of the Eastern Church* 1957, pp. 8–9
21. I John 1:1 ff
22. Lossky. op. cit., p. 42
23. ibid., p. 39

4

Ann Griffiths, Mystic and Theologian

I

The celebration in 1976 of the bi-centenary of Ann Griffiths's birth aroused new interest in her work not only in Wales, where she has always been remembered as one of the most striking figures in the Methodist revival, but also in the English-speaking world, where as yet she is scarcely a name. Something of the special quality of her work, its deeply theological and experiential character, has begun to be more clearly seen. Anyone who reads Ann Griffiths's hymns soon perceives that she is a lover of paradox.[1] By use of contradictions, or at least apparent contradictions, she seeks to lead us further into the understanding of the mysteries to which she draws our attention. But she herself is also something of a contradiction. We say that she is a theologian and a mystic. But was she not a high-spirited, hard-working farmer's daughter in a remote part of mid-Wales? In what sense can she be a theologian? And is it not a fact that there is an incompatibility between the Calvinist theology which she had learnt and any mystical form of Christianity? Many of the most eminent Protestant scholars of our century have thought so.

These are some of the questions which we shall be encountering. I shall hope to show, to anticipate my conclusion, that Ann was indeed a mystic and a theologian and that far from being the one at the expense of the other it was precisely because she was a theologian that she was such a notable mystic, precisely because she was a mystic that she was such a notable theologian.

II

When Morris Davies composed his *Cofiant* in 1865, the first
thorough investigation of her life and work, he was already aware of
the problem involved in her being a theologian, though he saw it
rather differently from the way in which we should. That she is a
theologian he has no doubt. 'We see the unrestrained, frivolous
young woman, who was to the fore in all kinds of social evenings and
dance parties ... as if at once changed into an "accomplished
theologian" with clear and wide views on the teachings of the Gospel
in their excellence and coherence.'[22] For him, what is surprising is
the moral transformation involved. For us this is unlikely to be such
a problem. For one thing we shall probably be less impressed than he
was by the wickedness of Ann's light-hearted escapades. For another
we may be inclined to think that a childhood spent with a father as
generous and good-natured as John Evan Thomas seems to have
been, a childhood in which there was ample opportunity to become
familiar with the Bible and the Book of Common Prayer, was not in
itself such a bad preparation for becoming a theologian. What is
more likely to amaze us is the sudden revelation of unexpected
intellectual capacities in one with so little formal education. That
someone with only two years of schooling who, judged by the one
surviving manuscript letter, did not know of the existence of punc-
tuation, should show such a grasp of intricate theological questions
is for us with our fixed presuppositions about the necessity of education at least as startling as the moral transformation was for our
nineteenth-century predecessors.

A comparison, taken from the other end of Europe, may be
illuminating here. In our own days, the writings of the Staretz
Silouan, a monk of the Russian monastery on Mount Athos who died
in 1938, have become well known through translation into a
number of Western languages, and admired as much for their
theological precision as for their spiritual beauty.[3] Like Ann, the
Staretz had only two years' schooling, in his case in a village school
in the central Russian province of Tambov in the 1870s, where I
doubt whether the standards were any higher than were those of Mrs
Owen Y Sais at Dolanog a hundred years before. In his case, as in

that of Ann, a life of profound prayer and faith released possibilities of balanced and lucid theological statement which might well make a 'professor' of theology envious. Certainly for such people as the Staretz and Ann some knowledge of the sources, in the Bible and in the Liturgy, is essential. But the experience out of which they speak is not gained only or even primarily by the reading of books. The Christian tradition of faith and understanding has a power of renewing itself from within, in those who live the things they believe in, in ways which escape our usual methods of historical investigation. Such people are, we may say, taught of God; or if we prefer, we may say that the images which they handle have such an inherent power that they tend to come alive of themselves. That is why, though it would be most valuable to make a detailed study of the books which Ann might have read, such a line of research would not reveal all the secrets of her greatness. A purely academic approach to such writing is likely, in the end, to leave us feeling unsatisfied.

For while it must be evident to anyone who reads Ann Griffiths with an eye to her theology that she had a firm grasp of the fundamental articles of Christian faith as well as of the doctrines particularly favoured in the movement to which she belonged, it must also be evident that she was a woman of powerful feeling and imagination, whose whole being was moved by the nature of the things which she believed. 'Her longing was ardent, passionate, heavenly; her rejoicing and delight [in the things of God] sometimes almost unbelievable.'[4] There was that combination of intellectual vision and heartfelt longing in her which we find in nineteenth-century France in a Sister Elizabeth of the Trinity, in sixteenth-century Spain in a St Theresa of Avila. 'Oh thou undaunted daughter of desires . . . by all thy dower of lights and fires . . . by thy large draughts of intellectual day, and by the thirsts of love more large than they . . .' (terms which Crashaw addressed to St Theresa). The power of this yearning after God disturbed Morris Davies. Had it not been for her firm grounding in evangelical doctrine, he fears that it might have led her towards Popery and superstition; she might, he remarks, have become the abbess of a convent. Though we may well have a very different estimate of Roman Catholicism from his, we see what he means and must surely agree with him when he concludes that what is so notable in her is the combination of heart and head, of feeling and intellect. 'There was both light and warmth in her religion. Not heat without light, nor light without heat, but the two joined together.'[5]

And here we are already plunged into the question of mysticism. For although Morris Davies never mentions the word—it was indeed scarcely used in its modern sense in the mid-nineteenth century in English nor, I imagine, in Welsh—this longing for union with the divine is one of the features which are common to mystical religion wherever we find it. For, of course, it may be found far beyond the bounds of Christendom. This fact provides one of the reasons why mysticism has been particularly suspect to many of the most eminent Protestant thinkers of our day, for they have wished at all costs to maintain the uniqueness of Christian faith over against the religions of mankind. For them mysticism has been judged to be an alien element within the Christian tradition. In Wales this point of view was maintained with great skill and learning by the late Professor J. R. Jones, who argued that in Ann the theological and mystical elements were both present, but ultimately unreconciled.

This is not the place to examine in any detail the two sides of this argument about mysticism. For myself, it seems to do more justice to the facts to recognise that there is a mystical element in Christianity which is to be found not only in the Catholic tradition of the Christian East and West, but also in classical Protestantism itself, especially in the seventeenth and eighteenth centuries.[6] This is not the mysticism of identity, which characterises much of Hinduism and Buddhism, in which the soul seeks to realise its identity with the source of all being. It is the mysticism of loving communion, of personal relationship, which in various forms is to be found in Judaism and Islam, as well as in Christianity. It is to this tradition that Ann belongs, and she displays many of its most typical and constant features.

Let us turn now to her letters to examine in more detail two recurrent themes, which help us to understand the nature of this longing after God. The first I shall call 'going beyond', the second 'entering in'. We may in passing remark that both are typical of the Christian tradition of spirituality wherever we may find it. The first theme refers to the longing to go beyond all created things to God himself. In the second letter to John Hughes, Ann writes: 'A thought has struck me . . . on the passage, "Simon, son of Jonas, lovest thou me more than these?" I thought that we have to pass beyond brethren and graces, and love the Giver above the gift.'[7] In the following letter she takes up the same subject in relation to the Old Testament story about Moses appointing elders to give judgement in lesser cases, while reserving the principal matters to himself. Then with reference to the 'watchers' in the *Song of Songs*, Ann says 'I have thought that in my perplexing situation it is necessary to pass beyond the watchers of the city and everything else, to God alone.'[8] It is interesting to note that this way of interpreting the *Song of Songs* has been common to many writers of earlier centuries of whom Ann can have had no knowledge.

In the sixth letter, the same point is made in a slightly different context.

> Another word was a special blessing to me lately when I tried to speak to the Lord about the various things which were calling me to go after them. This is the word, 'Look unto me, all the ends of the earth, that ye may be saved, for I am God, and not another.' As if God were saying, I know about all the things that call to you, and how various they are, but I myself am calling. The world is only the world, the flesh is only the flesh, and the devil is only the devil, it is I who am God, and no one else.[9]

The transcendent and imperious power of God's call is here forcibly stated. We see something of the way in which Ann made the Calvinist insistence on the sovereignty and majesty of God her own. In this context, we can better understand many of the apparently negative expressions of the hymns. It is not that Ann is tired of this world. She has seen something else, which has wholly captured her attention. 'The world and all its toys, cannot now satisfy my affections, which have been captured, which have been widened in the day of the power of my great Jesus; he, and nothing less, can fill them, incomprehensible though he is—O to gaze upon his Person, man and God as he is' (18).[10]

The last two lines of this verse bring us naturally to our second theme, which I have called 'entering in' and at once remind us of the fact that with Ann, it is impossible to separate experience from theology. She longs to enter into the closest possible communion with God, and to remain constant in it. But this communion is opened to her only in the person of Christ. As Morris Davies so rightly remarks, 'The Mediator was the central point of her whole system. He was the Alpha and Omega of her salvation and her blessedness . . .'[11]

But let us see how Ann herself expresses it. In the second letter to John Hughes we have this: 'It occurred to me that I should be content to give all that I possess, be it good or evil, to possess the Son, in a marriage union.'[12] The image of the marriage union does not occur again in the letters but the thought of giving all, and the desire to enter into constant communion with God in his Son, recurs in each of the last three letters in the series.

'But this I will say deliberately, I desire that the remaining part of my life should be in communion so close that it might never again belong to me to say: 'I will go and I will return.' So she writes in the fifth letter, and in the following one: 'I should heartily wish to give all the praise to God the Word, simply for leading me and upholding me so far, and that what remains of my life should be spent in abiding communion with God in his Son, because I never can glorify him more than, or as much as, by believing in and accepting his Son. Heaven help me to do this . . .'[13]

This same prayer is made even more insistently in the next letter. 'But here is my trouble—failing to abide—continually departing. O for help to abide.'[14] This theme finds its fullest expression in the letter to Elizabeth Evans, in which she speaks of the need to give herself up to God 'daily and continually, body and soul'[15], surely one of the unforgettable passages in Ann's prose. But this is a letter which we shall examine later.

III

All this, it may be said, shows that Ann had a great longing after

God, but is this of itself enough to qualify her as a mystic, or a contemplative? Is the constant stress which we find in her letters on the element of conflict, on the alternations of hope and fear, consistent with one who has made any serious advance in the spiritual way? Where should we place her in terms of the three stages of spiritual life commonly discerned in the Catholic tradition, the purgative, the illuminative and the unitive?

The question is one which in this form we cannot answer. What is clear from the letters and hymns alike is that she knew much in her experience of the elements of purgation and illumination. She speaks of the longing to be pure which the heavenly vision awakes in her, and of her willingness to bear the sufferings which lead towards this simplification and clarity of vision. That there is illumination here is abundantly evident, not from the hymns only but from the majestic paragraph in letter V, where she comments on the text from the *Song of Songs*, 'Go forth, O ye daughters of Zion, and behold King Solomon with the crown wherewith his mother crowned him in the day of his espousals, and in the day of the gladness of his heart.' And here, as in other places, there is not only the imaginative vision but also the intuitive understanding, that we are to be called out of our 'ceiled houses', our own small worlds of images and concepts, to see the King in the incomprehensible glory of his offering of himself for us. The very strength of the longing after union with God expressed in the passages which we have been considering suggests that their author already knew much of what it was that she desired. 'You would not seek me unless you had already found me.'

On the place of inner strife and conflict in the spiritual life it may be useful to cite by way of comparison an author of an earlier century, Isaac of Stella, one of the outstanding figures of the first generation of the Cistercian reform. Coming from one whose standing within a classical moment in the history of Christian spirituality is not in question, it will suggest that Ann's complaint about her 'failure to abide' is not necessarily to be accepted at its face value.

I am visited at dawn, and then suddenly abandoned; no sooner I am raised up, than I find myself deserted; I am carried forward and immediately cast down, like a man who walks through the mountains without finding any sure path. Sometimes I am filled

with joy and songs of praise, bathed in an excess of light and
pierced by a wonderful sweetness, exulting in the unspeakable
hope of a salvation I had not expected; everything encourages me,
all the signs are favourable, there is no more room for doubt, it is
as if I had already attained the goal. Sometimes I am filled with
anxieties and tears, enveloped in darkness and full of bitterness, I
am eaten up with such a confusion of disgust and boredom, that
everything seems to deny my hopes and constrains me to silence.
Woe to the wretched man who cannot join himself to God as he
would wish to do, nor stand firm in his own purposes. For myself,
I must confess, I never stand firm in myself. I am incessantly
ground between hope and fear. . . . The grace of God always
enables me to find some cause for hope in myself. The 'me' in
myself constantly makes me find some cause for fear. At one
moment I grasp all that I hope for; at the next I lose all that I had
grasped. . . .[16]

The only recourse for the Cistercian abbot, as for the farmer's daughter, is to cry more strongly to the Lord. As George Herbert comments in the seventeenth century,

> These are thy wonders, Lord of power,
> Killing and quick'ning, bringing down to hell
>   And up to Heaven in an hour;
> Making a chiming of a passing bell.
>   We say amiss
>   This or that is
> Thy word is all if we could spell.[17]

We have said earlier that reading alone will not make an Ann
Griffiths. But clearly for her, reading, and before all else Bible
reading, was vitally important. The Bible provided the objective
point of reference against which her inner experience could be
tested. The work of the mind must be joined to that of the heart,
and both alike must feel the impulse of God's Spirit on the human
spirit.

It is remarkable that in speaking of the way in which Ann became at home in the mysteries of the faith, Morris Davies speaks of the three elements in the life of personal prayer which have been classical in monastic practice from the middle ages until today, *lectio, meditatio, oratio.* Speaking of her attitude towards the mysteries of the faith, he says: 'The excellence and clarity of her compositions shows her clearly to have been a woman who greatly loved reading and meditation.'[18] And a little further on he speaks no less clearly of the importance for her of 'secret prayer'. Only in meditation and prayer can the mysteries be assimiliated, become part of ourselves to such a degree that we find we are becoming part of them. In his essay in the *Cofiant* of 1865, Caledfryn contrasts the superficial preaching of his own day with the kind of preaching which had been charac- teristic of an earlier generation, whose power had come 'not from a beautiful appearance, nor from strength of voice, nor from quantity of matter, nor from all these things together, but from the anointing which comes through prayer, and through constant meditation on the divine truth.'[19]

There are few points at which we come closer to Ann than in the stories which tell something of that hidden prayer of the heart which was hers. We hear of her retiring to the outhouse, sometimes many times in one day, in order to have solitude and silence to pursue this inward converse with the Lord. We hear of her sitting at the spin- ning wheel, the Bible open on a little table beside her, the tears streaming down her cheeks. We hear of moments of exaltation when she could not contain the audible expression of joy, we hear of nights of testing when she would wake up Ruth, to share her overwhelming sense of nearness of eternity and judgement. If Isaac of Stella, with all the resources of the monastic tradition around him, in common life and prayer, in spiritual discernment and advice, frequently found himself at a loss to understand his inner turmoil, how much greater must her need have been. We need not be surprised if there is sometimes a sense of strain in her. She tells us little about this secret prayer, but what she tells us is all important, and it is con- stantly pointing to what Caledfryn calls the 'anointing', the touch of God's Spirit on man's spirit, there in the inmost place of the heart. This is particularly true in the letter to Elizabeth Evans, where we find indications about prayer and the work of the Spirit which bring us to the centre both of her theology and her experience. But before we examine the letter in detail, let us look again for a moment at her view of the faith as a whole.

Morris Davies is certainly right in saying, as we have already seen, that the person and work of the mediator, Jesus Christ, is the very heart and centre of her vision. It is he who being at once truly God and truly man brings together eternity and time, the creature and the Creator. By his death he enables the Father freely to forgive, while holding the Law in honour. In his resurrection and ascension, the way for us is opened into the heavenly places, where he ever lives to make intercession. In her hymns she never ceases to sing the praise of his person in whom there is union without confusion, distinction without separation. But there are other doctrines which, though less in evidence, are scarcely less vital to her thought. Morris Davies enumerates them, and it is interesting to see what he puts first, 'As we read her compositions, we get clear proof that her thoughts were at home in the glorious mystery of the Trinity of persons in the Godhead, the union of the two natures in the eternal Son of God, the divinity and work of the Holy Spirit. . . .'[20] In relation to the doctrines of the Trinity and the Incarnation it is important to remark that both were formulated in the earliest Christian centuries, when there was no thought of an opposition between mysticism and theology—and that both make use of the concepts of union without confusion, and distinction without separation. These concepts, I should maintain, were developed not for the sake of intellectual subtlety but as responding to a profound experience of man's relationship with God, and of his relationship with other men, an experience of mutual indwelling.[21] 'He that abideth in love, abideth in God and God in him.' This is why they had so powerful an attraction for Ann; they enable her to speak about the love of God, and about the God who is love.

For her, the doctrine of the Trinity was particularly associated with her conviction that the love which God has for us is a love which has existed from all eternity within the life of God himself. 'Sweet it is to remember the Covenant that was made yonder by Three in One, to gaze eternally upon the Person who took the nature of man. . .'(27²).[22] And again: ' . . . Here are the foundations of the second covenant, here is the counsel of the Three in One, here is the wine which is able to cheer, to cheer the heart of God and man'

(8⁴).²³ In this assurance that the salvation of man is rooted in the
eternal counsel of the Three in One, Ann is not alone among the
hymn writers of her time. We may remember the striking lines of
Pedr Fardd (Peter Jones, 1775–1845): 'Before earth was made, or
the bright heavens stretched out, before the sun or the moon or the
stars were placed above, a way was set forth in the counsel of the
Three in One, for the salvation of poor, lost guilty man.' In these
hymns of Welsh Methodism we have a verbal equivalent of the
greatest of Russian icons, the Old Testament Trinity of Andrei
Rublev, in which the three persons are seen seated around a table, on
which stands the cup of sacrifice, the symbol of self-giving love.

But for Ann this doctrine stands not only at the beginning of all
things, but also at their fulfilment. It is through this doctrine that
she is able to look forward to that final participation in the life and
love of God, in which the separation between human and divine is
overcome but in which what is created is not simply annihilated.
'Abundant freedom of entrance, ever to continue, into the dwelling
places of the Three in One, water to swim in, not to be passed
through, man as God and God as man'(7⁴).²⁴ As we read these texts
we may well agree with Morris Davies, that Ann's mind was 'at
home' in these things. She handles them with all the assurance of a
master.

IV

It is against such a background of Trinitarian faith and experience,
that we come to understand the full meaning of what Ann says in the
letter to Elizabeth Evans, about the doctrine of the Holy Spirit. It is
because this doctrine is so vital to her that any distortion of it is
bound to be felt as at once painful and deeply harmful.

Dear Sister, the most outstanding thing that is on my mind at
present as a matter for thought has to do with grieving the Holy
Spirit. The word came into my mind, 'Know ye not that your
bodies are temples of the Holy Ghost which dwelleth in you?'
And on penetrating a little into the wonder of the Person, and
how he dwells or resides in the believer, I think in short that I

have never been possessed to the same degree by reverential fears of grieving him, and along with this I have been able to see one reason, and the chief reason, why this great sin has made such a slight impression and weighed so lightly upon my mind, on account of my base and blasphemous thoughts about a Person so great.

This is how my thoughts ran about the Persons of the Trinity. I feel my mind being seized by shame, and even inhibited from speaking on account of the harmfulness of this. I thought of the Persons of the Father and the Son as co-equal; but as for the Person of the Holy Spirit, I regarded him as a functionary subordinate to them. O what a misguided imagination about a Person who is divine, all-present, all-knowing, and all-powerful to carry on and complete the good work which he has begun in accordance with the covenant of grace, and the counsel of the Three in One regarding those who are the objects of the primal love. O for the privilege of being one of their number.[25]

Ever since I first read the text of Ann's letters in the translation of Evan Richards, I have been greatly struck by the force with which she confesses her error in Trinitarian theology. With her extraordinary capacity to state much in little, she sums up in the phrase describing the Holy Spirit as a 'functionary subordinate to' the other two persons of the Trinity, a tendency which has marked the thinking and devotion of Catholics and Protestants alike for many centuries, and which certainly must have affected her. As in other places where she reproaches herself, we need to be on our guard, for while we should certainly take her seriously, we should beware of taking her altogether literally. Doubtless she had at this time received a new and overwhelming impression of the reality of the person and work of the third person of the Holy Trinity. But faith in the indwelling of the Holy Spirit in the believer was not wholly new to her. In the third letter to John Hughes she had written '. . . let us often entreat that the Holy Spirit may make his home in us.'[26]

But even so, how are we to take these extreme expressions of distress over what would seem to most people, a small error about a remote doctrinal matter? Certainly there is the outpouring of a devout and perhaps over-sensitive heart and mind. But is there more than that? I believe that there is, and I believe that I can now perceive what it is.

Ann not only had a vivid sense of the meaning of particular doctrines, she also had an intuitive grasp of the coherence of the different elements of Christian belief, the way in which they fit together. Now faith in the person and work of the Holy Spirit, the belief that he is truly God and that he is truly present in us, is the necessary fulfilment and complement of faith that in Jesus Christ, God and man are indeed reconciled and at one. Without it, the former article is incomplete. As Lancelot Andrewes put it, in his first sermon for Whitsunday: 'without either of them we are not complete, we have not our accomplishment.' For we are made at one with God not only through the union of the two natures in the person of the Son, but also through the communion of divine with human in the coming of the Holy Spirit, in his dwelling in us. *Incarnatio Dei,* says Andrewes, is completed in *Inspiratio hominis,* 'whereby, as before He of ours, so now we of His are made partakers. He clothed with our flesh, we invested with His Spirit.'[27] The whole work of grace is truncated, cut short, if we do not make this final step. In particular, all the 'sanctifying' influences of the Gospel on those who believe, to fit them to glorify God in this world, and to enjoy him for ever in the world to come'[28] are weakened and deprived of their source and centre unless seen as flowing from the person and work of the Holy Spirit.

All this Ann has seen; all this she wishes to repair. Hence in her letter having confessed her faith in the divinity of the Holy Spirit she goes on at once to pray that she may know his presence and activity in her own life in all its details.

> Dear Sister, I feel a degree of thirst to grow up more in the belief in the personal indwelling of the Holy Spirit in my life; and this by way of revelation, not of my own imagination, as if I thought to comprehend in what way or by what means it happens, which is real idolatry.

And knowing her fallen condition and her inability to do anything of herself in this matter, she turns to prayer as her only resource. In particular she speaks

... about the virtue of secret prayer ... I know from experience through finding myself surrounded by enemies, that I could find nothing to say but this,—'And I give myself unto prayer'; and this answers the purpose of making them fall back. O for the privilege of being under the detailed supervision of the Holy Spirit; I think quite simply that my condition will never be met by a supervision less detailed than is expressed in this word, 'I will water it every moment.'[29]

We have said that in this letter Anns speaks as a master of spiritual things, a doctor of faith and theology, one who teaches of such things from experience and vision. But she also speaks as a simple believer, one who seeks to realise these things in her own life. It is in the same letter that she speaks most simply of the demands of the vision in her life.

Dear Sister, I see more need than ever to spend my remaining days in giving myself up daily and continually, body and soul, into the care of him who is able to keep that which is committed unto him against that day. Not to give myself once, but to live continually giving myself, right up to and in the very moment when I put away this tabernacle. Dear sister, the thought of putting it away is particularly sweet sometimes, I can say that this is what cheers me more than anything else in these days, not death in itself, but the great gain that is to be got through it. To be able to leave behind every inclination that goes against the will of God, to leave behind every ability to dishonour the law of God, with all weakness swallowed up by strength, to become fully conformed to the law which is already on one's heart and to enjoy God's likeness for ever. Dear sister, I am sometimes absorbed so far into these things that I completely fail to stand in the way of my duty with regard to temporal things, but I look for the time when I may find release and be with Christ, for that is much better, although it is very good here through a lattice, and the Lord sometimes reveals through a glass, darkly, as much of his glory as my weak faculties can bear.[30]

Surely, on any showing the letter to Elizabeth Evans for all its brevity must stand as one of the great documents in the history of Christian spirituality. In its own simplicity it stands above the divisions between mysticism and theology, bearing witness to the fact that, as Vladimir Lossky says: 'there is no Christian mysticism without theology; but above all, there is no theology without mysticism.'[31]

Ann in her lifetime was baptised, married and buried in the church of her parish at Llanfihangel-yng-Ngwynfa. Although she later broke with it, it was there and in her home that she received her first nurturing in spiritual things. Her awakening and conversion began under the auspices of the Independents, her continued growth was dependent on the Calvinistic Methodists and it is to their family that she primarily belongs. In our own century, she has exercised a particular attraction for her Roman Catholic fellow-countrymen, who have seen in her something of the character of their own great contemplative saints. If, as has been suggested here, she has also a deep affinity with Eastern Orthodoxy, then she may indeed prove to be a truly catholic figure, who can draw Christians of many traditions into one. And why only Christians? Surely the things that were seen and done in the brief lifetime at Dolwar Fachan, however we interpret them, can speak, in some way, to all men, and help all who will to have a deeper vision of human life, to recognise that our human condition in all its frailty and limitation is sometimes visited by strange and heavenly powers.

What is life? Finding a large room
Between narrow walls.[32]

Within the brief compass of her life and the narrow confines which contained it, Ann had indeed found a large space. And we too, through her work, no less limited in its outward range, can find an inner space of immeasurable riches, a place where heaven and earth, eternity and time, are at one.

NOTES

1. A brief account of the life of Ann Griffiths can be found in my book on her in The Writers of Wales Series, published by the University of Wales Press. A verse translation of the hymns can be found in H. A. Hodges, *Homage to Ann Griffiths*, Church in Wales Publications, 1976
2. Morris Davies. *Cofiant Ann Griffiths* (in Welsh), Dinbych, 1865, p. 53
3. Archimandrite Sofrony. *The Undistorted Image; Staretz Sylvan, 1866–1938*, London, 1958, republished in two volumes as *The Monk from Mount Athos*, and *Wisdom from Mount Athos*
4. Morris Davies. op. cit., p. 56
5. ibid., p. 57
6. cf. e.g. Louis Bouyer. *Orthodox Spirituality and Protestant and Anglican Spirituality*, London, 1969, pp. 58–62
7. O. M. Edwards. *Gwaith Ann Griffiths* (in Welsh), Conwy, 1905, p. 9. All the translations of passages from Ann's letters and hymns are the work of H. A. Hodges
8. ibid., p. 13
9. ibid., p. 18
10. ibid., p. 38
11. Morris Davies. op. cit., p. 53
12. O. M. Edwards. op. cit., pp. 9–10
13. ibid., p. 19
14. ibid., p. 21
15. ibid., p. 25
16. Isaac de l'Etoile. *Sermons*, Vol. II (Sources Chrétiennes), Paris, 1974, pp. 177–9.
17. *The Works of George Herbert*, ed. F. E. Hutchinson, Oxford, p. 166
18. Morris Davies. op. cit., p. 52
19. ibid., p. 151
20. ibid., p. 53
21. cf. George Every in *New Heaven? New Earth? An Encounter with Pentecostalism*, 1976, pp. 171–2:
   'It seems to be a mistake to think of the doctrine of the Incarnation as arising simply out of reflection on the historical evidence for the life of Christ in the gospels, without regard to the communion of Christians in his risen life, to their sense of the relationship between his humanity in the heavenly places and our own, between our resurrection and his, as this was perceived through participation in baptism and the Eucharist, and through the whole life of Christians at prayer in Christ and in the Spirit. In the same way the doctrine of the Trinity arises out of prayer in the Spirit to the Father through Jesus Christ our Lord. This is not a consequence but a cause of the formulation of the doctrine. . . . The vision of the Trinity arises out of Trinitarian prayer, and not out of metaphysical speculation, although Christians took part in this with other philosophers of the time. . . .'
22. O. M. Edwards. op. cit., p. 43

23. ibid., p. 31
24. ibid., p. 30
25. ibid., p. 23
26. ibid., p. 13
27. *The Works of Lancelot Andrews*, (LACT) Vol. III, Oxford, 1854, p. 109
28. Morris Davies. op. cit., p. 54
29. O. M. Edwards. op. cit., p. 24
30. ibid., p. 26
31. V. Lossky. *The Mystical Theology of the Eastern Church*, London, 1958, p. 9.
32. Waldo Williams. *Dail Pren* (in Welsh), Aberystwyth, 1956, p. 67

5

N. F. S. Grundtvig: the Spirit as Life-giver

The name of N. F. S. Grundtvig is scarcely known outside his own native country. Except amongst those who are interested in the Scandinavian system of adult education, his work is simply ignored. And this is itself a highly significant fact. We could find various reasons for it. Danish is not a language widely read outside Scandinavia. The activity and life of Grundtvig were so inextricably entwined with the life of his own small nation that they have seemed to many outsiders to be of scarcely more than national interest; I suspect that this may be one of the reasons why the Germans have paid so little attention to him. His style certainly is difficult and his works are so voluminous that it is difficult to know where to begin. But behind these factors there lies another and profounder one, which I believe to be more important, and more directly relevant to the purpose of this study. Grundtvig is above all a theologian, but not in the sense in which that word has been understood in the last two centuries in Western Christendom. He will not fit into our categories, ecclesiastical or academic. We need to understand him against the background of an older and larger definition of theology.

'A theologian is one who prays truly. One who prays truly is a theologian.'[1] This ancient monastic saying proves surprisingly true in the case of Grundtvig. I do not by this mean to imply that there was anything monastic in his way of living the Christian life. Married three times, for more than sixty years involved in every kind of activity and controversy, intellectual, social, political, ecclesiastical, Grundtvig is the very type of the man engaged in the life of his time and place, who finds God in and through his creation not apart from it. But if we wish to find the heart of his teaching we must look not to his polemical writings or his pamphlets, but to his sermons and still more to his hymns. His is a theology of praise and proclamation. He created a body of liturgical hymns, hymns for the festivals and for the sacraments, which are without parallel in Protestant Christendom. His is a theology, moreover, which is expressed primarily in images and not in concepts. The image language of the Bible and the Fathers—and especially of the Fathers in their capacity as preachers and men of prayer—came to life again in nineteenth-century Denmark through his work.

This did not happen by chance. Like all those involved in the romantic movement, a movement which greatly influenced him in his youth, Grundtvig was in reaction against the shallow rationalism which had dominated Europe in the eighteenth century. He was no less concerned to combat both the drily scholastic theology of the earlier Lutheran orthodoxy and the newly found intellectualism of the religious thinkers of nineteenth-century Germany. To an eager disciple of Hegel discoursing of the nature of thesis and antithesis, Grundtvig replied: 'My antithesis is life and death.' As a preacher and teacher Grundtvig was always concerned with the living word, whether spoken or sung, that is to say with the word as it expresses and directs the lives of men and women. He was concerned to speak to the whole man, body, soul and spirit, and it is not surprising that one of the key terms alike in his hymns and in his sermons, is the word 'heart'. This is a word which holds a considerable place in the teaching of Old and New Testament, and is essential for understanding the patristic view of human nature. It speaks of a centre in men where feeling and thought, intuition and will are fused together into one. As a recent Danish writer on the meaning of the word 'heart', in Grundtvig's thought, drily remarks, it is scarcely to be found as a significant term in modern dogmatic or specialist theology. There could scarcely be a sharper condemnation of the theology of our time, or a clearer indication of one of the reasons why it seems to many, believers as well as unbelievers, an irrelevance.

In the course of a long life Grundtvig's theological position underwent a number of changes. Perhaps the most important of all was what he himself called 'the unparalleled discovery' of the years 1823 and 1824. This involved, first and foremost, a discovery of the power of the living Christ at work now and through all the centuries in the Church's life and worship. Suddenly Grundtvig saw that it was not possible to build the Church on the Bible, but that rather it was necessary to place the Bible in the Church, in fact to place it on the altar. It is through the sacraments of Baptism and Eucharist in which we hear God's word to us, that the life of the Church of Christ is built up. It is here, together with the baptismal confession of faith in the apostles' creed and the celebration of the great festivals of Christmas, Easter and Whitsun, that the essential marks of the Church are to be found. Already we can see the ecumenical implications of Grundtvig's discovery emerging, for these are precisely things which unite Christians across their divisions. In Grundtvig's first attempt at a systematic statement of his new position, *The Church's Rejoinder, Kirkens Gienmaele,* a work which he dated from St Irenaeus's Day, 1825, the ecumenical nature of his appeal to the one historical Church of Christ becomes clearly evident.

If the 1820s were marked for Grundtvig by this overwhelming discovery of the living continuity of the Church in prayer and sacrament, the 1830s involved for him a new appreciation of the doctrine of creation, and of the place of this world in God's plan of salvation. More and more he came to see a dynamic interaction between the work of Christ and the Spirit in redemption, and the work of Christ and the Spirit in creation. So powerful was his teaching in this area that his theology touched the social and political life of his nation in a way rare amongst nineteenth-century theologians. But this increased awareness of the work of God in creation, did not result in any lessening of his sense of the creative activity of God in the Church's worship. Quite the reverse; it was in 1836 that he began to publish his great collection of hymns, *Sang Vaerk til den Danske Kirke,* and to these years some of the finest of them belong. I think specially of the hymns celebrating Sunday as the day of the resurrection and the coming of the Spirit, and of the hymns written specifically for Pentecost. Even in translation something of their splendour can be perceived.

This is the day which the Lord has made,
This day rejoices his servants.
This day he opened the gate of Heaven,
This shall each Sunday resound.
For in these thrice-holy hours
Glorious from death God's Word arose
Gracious from Heaven God's Spirit came down.
Now do you see why the bells ring?[2]

Or again

Awake all deep voices
To praise the Redeemer of mankind;
Be gathered together all languages
In the sacrificial cup of thanksgiving.
Sound out over the Lord's table
The full choir of God's people.

In Jesus's Name where tongues catch fire
Amongst gentiles as amongst Jews,
In the sacrificial cup of Jesus's name
All mother-tongues fuse into one,
In Jesus's Name there bursts forth
the eternal Halleluja.[3]

I

What was the structure of thought which lay behind such ecstatic
utterances? In answering that question I shall refer to a series of
excellent studies of major themes in Grundtvig's sermons and hymns
produced by a group of young scholars working under the direction
of Professor Christian Thodberg in the University in Aarhus, and
published in the autumn of 1977. These essays, which make extensive use of the unpublished texts of many of the sermons, are excep-
tionally helpful in elucidating some of the basic lines along which

Grundtvig's thought developed.[4] Let us then start from the central point, the doctrine of God.

In expounding the doctrine of the Holy Trinity the first thing that we notice is that in contrast to much Western Trinitarian theology, Grundtvig begins by putting the emphasis on the three. The term which he uses in Danish is Tri-Unity, *Tre-Enighed.* One of the greatest of contemporary Danish theologians, Regin Prenter, in most things an admirer of Grundtvig, even accuses him of a certain tendency towards tri-theism. The three persons are united in one nature, one will, one love, a love which Grundtvig remarks is infinitely deeper than that between even the most united husband and wife. And as there are millions of men and women united in one human nature, so the three persons are united in one divine nature. In this unity of the three persons, we see the distinctive Christian vision of God. Preaching on Trinity Sunday, 1833, Grundtvig can speak of the 'God of the Christians, who is neither like the heathen's, a multitude of various self-made gods, nor like the Mohammedan's, a single God the Father, without Son or Spirit, unknowable and lifeless, impossible and self-contradictory, but is the holy Tri-Unity.'[5] We are at once led to think of the similar remark of St Gregory Nazianzen distinguishing the Christian concept of God from that of the multiplicity of the Greeks and the unity of the Jews.

How in such a view of things does Grundtvig assure the unity of the Godhead? Precisely as do the Greek Fathers, by stressing the monarchy of the Father. Basing himself on I Corinthians 8:6, 'there is one God, the Father, of whom are all things . . .', Grundtvig constantly stresses that it is the Father who is the unique source of deity. Hence in his hymns he can use the language of Irenaeus and speak of the Son and the Spirit as the two hands of God; this incidentally in a hymn which celebrates our Lord's baptism as the revelation of God's inner nature. Morten Mortenson sums up his teaching thus: 'The Father is the only one who exists of and by himself; both the Son and the Spirit have their existence from and by the Father, even though in all else they are equal with him and co-eternal with him.' In his preaching about the Trinity Grundtvig lays great weight on the names, Father, Son, Spirit. 'What becomes evident here is Grundtvig's understanding that heavenly and divine realities and phenomena cannot be expressed in logical, discursive language, but can only be conveyed in images.'[6] Here again we see his dislike for the logically constructed Trinitarianism of scholastic theologians, and his preference for the theological method of Irenaeus.

For him the Father is the origin of all, the heart or the depth of deity. The Son, however, is subordinate to the Father only as Son. In all other things he is equal with him. Indeed he must be co-eternal, for only can the Father be Father if he has a Son. The Spirit is he who from all eternity proceeds from the Father. On this Grundtvig is perfectly clear. The Spirit who is sent by the Son, proceeds from the Father from all eternity. The language of the double procession, that the Spirit proceeds from the Father *and the Son,* is not to be found in him. Nor do we find the term *nexus amoris,* so common in Western theology, which speaks of the Holy Spirit as the bond of love, between Father and Son. Indeed if the word love is to be applied especially to any one of the Trinity, and clearly it belongs to all, for Grundtvig it would apply most appropriately to the Father who is the source of love. Of course Grundtvig in no way separates the Spirit from the Son; he constantly speaks of the reciprocal action between the two, in vigorous images, 'the power of the Spirit is the marrow of the Word . . . Word without Spirit is empty chatter, but Spirit without Word is vain imagination,'[7] but he insists no less on the real personhood of the Spirit and constantly combats any tendency to consider the Spirit as an impersonal power, or to make use of the pronoun 'it' rather than 'he' in relation to the Spirit. Furthermore he suggests that the knowledge of the Trinity given to each one of us in our baptism is something which is to deepen and grow through our constant participation in the life of the Trinity in the Holy Communion, and this growth is particularly the work of the Spirit. What is true of each one is also in some sense true of the Church; here, too, there is growth. Grundtvig has a very dynamic view of the history of the Church and of mankind, in which God is even now at work, unfolding what was once for all given in Christ.

We must indeed note that for him all three persons of the Trinity are at work from the first moment of creation till the fulfilment of all things. Jesus Christ, made man for us of Mary his mother, crucified and risen again, present with us in the font and at the altar, is the same Lord who has created all things in the beginning, in whose image and likeness man is made. The Holy Spirit by whom Jesus was conceived, descending on him in his Baptism, in whom he offered himself to the Father, descending upon the infant Church at Pentecost, is the same Spirit who moved on the face of the waters at creation, who is everywhere present and filling all things, the inspiration of all true love and knowledge in mankind, the life of all that has life throughout creation. There is throughout Grundtvig's teaching a remarkable stress on the interaction, *vekselvirkning*—it is one of his favourite terms—between creation and redemption, between universal and particular. We should not be able to see God at work everywhere in his world, unless we had been called out of death into life by the redeeming Word of Christ our Saviour. But we should not be able to hear that Word unless there was that in us which was created for God, that which, though darkened by the fall, so wounded as to be almost dead, could yet respond to the action of the Spirit. That man was made in God's image and likeness was for Grundtvig of all articles of the faith among the most essential. The heart of man is made to receive and respond to the love which comes from the heart of God. It is the place of the divine image within us. Erik Krebs Jensen sums up his teaching thus: 'The relationship between God and man is in its origin a loving father-child relationship. Man is of God's race, made by God's power to resemble God, a child in creation, full-grown in salvation.'[8] We may well be struck by the parallel with the words which St Seraphim is said to have heard in a vision from the Mother of God: 'He is of our race.'

Hence it is that for Grundtvig it is very important to recognise all that prepares for Christ's coming in the flesh. There is first of all the history recorded in the Old Testament. God chose out for himself a people, the people of Israel. The Spirit spoke by the prophets. Yes, the Spirit moved in the great figures of Israel's history, Abraham 'the hero of faith', John Baptist 'the angel of Hope', and Mary 'the Queen of the Heart', to use his own words, until finally there should be a place prepared for the coming of the Saviour. If we reflect for a moment on Grundtvig's understanding of the heart as the centre of man's being, as the receptive and responsive element in humanity, which is seen at its clearest and fullest in woman as mother, we see something of the weight to be attached to the term *Hjerte-Dronning*, (heart-Queen) which in him is far from being merely sentimental. As he says in one of his hymns, the responsive heart of mankind beat highest in the moment at which Mary received the angel's message and conceived by the Holy Ghost. But in Grundtvig the recognition of the particularity of God's call never blurs his vision of the universality of God's action. So he is anxious that we shall remember that every believer is called to be a Mary, that she is the type and representative of us all. We must not so isolate her as to make of her an earthly goddess.[9]

What is true of each one, is true also in some sense on a larger scale. The particularity of the call of Israel does not mean that all other nations are left outside the scope of God's providence. Every nation has some part, however obscure, in the preparation for the coming of Christ which was especially entrusted to Israel. Every people has its own spirit, which can respond in some way to the Spirit of God, a spirit which is conveyed through its own particular language, the vehicle of its own experience of life through the ages. Every people has its own inspired prophets and seers, as Grundtvig well knew having been one of the first to study the whole field of Norse mythology and legend. Of course, he does not simply equate the inspiration of poet or pagan bard, with the inspiraton of the prophets of Israel. There is need for a clear distinction. Very often the poet can give only a confused and confusing image of the heavenly country. His vision is often mixed with illusion. Yet everywhere the gift is to be found. Everywhere and in every tongue we find men and women who have been called to express something of the mystery of human existence, in its heights and its depths, to express some particular facet of the spirit which is in man.

This is true of the nations apart from Christ, before his coming. In them there is to be found some form of preparation for the Gospel, some longing for the revelation of the true destiny of man. It is, of course, still more true of the nations which have been baptised into him. Their spirit is truly moved by God's Spirit, so much so that at times we may be tempted to identify the one with the other. Grundtvig was aware of this temptation within himself, a temptation to believe that Denmark should become the spiritual Mary, 'who should conceive and bear Jesus anew, give new birth to his faith amongst all the peoples'.[10] If we are surprised at such words, let us remember rather similar sentiments expressed both in England and in Russia in the nineteenth century, both of which peoples had their temptations to thoughts of messianic grandeur. Do we suppose that God will choose large nations rather than small? The Bible would suggest the reverse. And let us not be too scornful. God does not disdain to dwell amongst men. The Spirit has not refused to speak through human lips. The words of men have become the vehicle of the Word of God; human languages have been hallowed by the gifts of the Spirit. All languages are potentially holy. This potentiality is realised when they are used to give voice to the praise of God's glory.

But ultimately of course, the gulf between creature and Creator remains. The Holy Spirit is not to be confused with man's spirit. No one nation, within the family of God, has a monopoly of the divine gift and calling. Rather at Pentecost we see that all peoples have their gift to contribute to the Catholic whole. All histories find their meaning in this history. All languages are united and fulfilled in this one sacrifice of praise. We see something of the depth of meaning in the lines already quoted;

> May all languages be gathered together
> In the sacrificial cup of thanksgiving
> (*I takkesangens offerskaal*
> *Forsamles alle tungemaal*)

and

> In the sacrificial cup of Jesus's name
> All mother-tongues fuse together.
> (*I Jesus-navnets offerskaal*
> *Hensmelter alle modersmaal.*)

As Saunders Lewis has put it, 'The mass makes sense of everything,' even the confusion of the tongues at Babel.

II

What is the particular action of the Holy Spirit in this? We may see it in Grundtvig under three main headings: First, growth, then elucidation, and third unification and fulfilment.

Grundtvig is a thinker for whom the concept of growth is of great importance. If very often he sees growth in terms of the history of mankind, in which God is constantly calling men into relationship with him, he does not in any way exclude the natural order from his vision of God's action. The great Pentecost hymn we have already cited begins with an evocation of summer and all the life and movement of the natural world. This is also the work of the one Holy Spirit. What is true of the world of nature, true of the history of nations, is true also of the history of each individual. The life of the Christian is also seen in terms of a constant growth under the influence of the Spirit. Our life in God begins in baptism, when the Spirit brings us to new birth in Christ, or rather, as Grundtvig loves to say, brings the Christ child to birth in us. The importance of baptism is primordial in Grundtvig's thought. Even the details of the baptismal rite are full of meaning for him. He makes much of the symbolism of the sign of the cross which the priest makes on the child's forehead and breast in the Danish rite. I quote again from Erik Kreb Jensen's essay on the heart of man as the place of the divine image.

> The fiery tongues of the Spirit with the sign of the cross burn the name of Jesus into the heart. Thus the heart encounters the stamp which corresponds to the image of God in the depths of the heart. The sign of the cross is a promise, a 'heavenly letter' about the operations of the new creation: faith, peace, hope and confidence, love and joy. It is basically a promise of Jesus's constant presence in the name which is on the heart, whence the Spirit can always lead us up to God in the word of faith.[11]

But of course our growth in Christian life is not uninterrupted or without difficulty. Constantly we have to recur to our baptism, constantly we need the Spirit's assistance as guide and comforter.

Grundtvig has a whole theology of prayer, based on the Lord's Prayer, which is given us in baptism. For him as for the teachers of the early Christian centuries it is the Lord's Prayer which provides the model. This is the way in which we grow in hope from baptism through the Eucharist towards the Kingdom, a Kingdom which is still to come, but which already we know by participation in the joy of the Church's worship, and whose signs we can see in the constant struggle of men and women in this world to construct a society corresponding more truly to the divine order. As we grow in faith and hope, and taste more deeply of that fullness of love which is given us in the Lord's Supper so also the Spirit's second work is carried forward, the work of elucidation.

Here we must interject a note of linguistic clarification. In Danish the word *forklare*, literally to make clear, means both explain and transfigure. *Forklaring* is explanation, *Forklarelse* is transfiguration. There is here something extraordinarily enlightening. On the one hand a good explanation is not something which 'explains away' the subject in hand, reducing it and making it banal. It is something which elucidates it, makes it clear, brings light to the matter. On the other hand, a moment of transfiguration, and *a fortiori* the moment of *the* Transfiguration, is not just a moment of ecstatic surprise, of amazement before the divine beauty. It is also a moment of enlightenment which casts its light backwards and forwards in time, which makes sense of much that otherwise is dark and apparently without meaning.

Grundtvig's vision of the world and man was certainly not one of unshadowed glory, nor was his own experience of life one of unbroken light. He knew times of deep darkness. He saw this world, and man within it, as full of riddles, *gaader*, mysteries. There is in man both light and darkness. And surely also in the being of God there are riddles too, mysteries which go beyond the reach of man's mind and yet correspond to something in the depths of the human heart. Grundtvig sought to express this vision both of God and of his creation. In so doing he used a language of images, which itself is sometimes full of mystery. The old man had enough of the *skjald* in him to delight in puzzling us with riddles. But such language, which may be dark to the intellect alone, can reveal itself to the heart, can become clear when it is met with the response of hope and love as well as with the intelligence of faith. This is one of the reasons why Grundtvig chose to express himself in hymns. He wished to speak to the whole congregation, to the uneducated, to women and to children, as well as to the educated to whom the sermon was too often addressed. His language of images is used to express the thoughts of our hearts, to appeal to our experience of life, in which thinking is only one element. The whole of human nature is to respond to the initiative of God. It is the work of the Holy Spirit to bring about this elucidation of the Word of God, as we meet him in the Scriptures, in the sacraments, in the Church's hymns of praise, so that the Lord himself may stand out before us transfigured in the splendour of his risen life. The presence of the risen Christ in the midst of his people together with the response of praise which this presence evokes, are expressed in Grundtvig's hymns with a power which I do not believe is to be found elsewhere in Protestantism. This is above all the work of the Spirit.

We have come to the final point of the Holy Spirit's work as I have sought to describe it here; *sammensmeltning,* unification, fusing together and fulfilment. Here again we must stand back a little if we are to appreciate all that this term came to mean in Grundtvig's heart and mind. As a young man, recently graduated from the University, too young and too immature to think of taking Holy Orders yet, he had gone as tutor to an aristocratic family in the country. There he fell desperately in love with his employer's wife. Not for the first time his heart was moved by feminine beauty. Suddenly the clever, discontented, young intellectual found his feelings, his imagination, and his mind coming to life. He discovered that he was a poet, he discovered that he had a calling, he discovered the writings of his great German contemporaries. It was the first decade of the nineteenth century. Under the influence of Schelling he came to think of the world around him as no more than a shadow, an image of an eternal and heavenly reality to which, occasionally the poet's genius might give him access. He felt, and was to feel all his life, an aching longing for that heavenly and eternal world which here we know only in shadows, shadows which are indeed most tantalising when they are most beautiful and apparently real.

What resolution was he to find to this mystery? Could there be any reconciliation of the heavenly with the earthly reality, any real meeting between the two contrasting worlds? Yes, he believed that he had found the answer. It was there in the coming of Christ in the flesh, in the Incarnation of the Word of God, in which the heavenly and eternal comes to meet us here in this world of time and change, and reveals to us in the power of the Spirit that this perishable world has its own value. It is more than merely a sign of another world; in some way it participates in the eternal reality which it mediates to us. He found that in the Incarnation of the Word, and in the presence of the indwelling Spirit, the two worlds had been fused into one. Not only the genius of the poet, but the faith of the ordinary believer could find the two united, could perceive the world in a grain of sand, and eternity in an hour, precisely because in Jesus the Word was made flesh. And Grundtvig received this knowledge with the whole of his being, a being which contained a mighty intellect—he was planning an edition of *Beowulf* before anyone in this country had begun to undertake it—with a great capacity for love—he shocked J. M. Neale on the occasion of their only meeting not so much because he had married again in his late sixties, after the death of his first wife, but because he was at that age so romantically and unashamedly in love.[12] Mind and heart had been fused together in the power of the Spirit, so that the heart could receive and respond to the revelation of God's glory.

As has already been suggested, for Grundtvig the Eucharist is a focal point in this fusion of the earthly and the heavenly, the place where the Spirit's work is most richly made known to us. In his youth he had reacted strongly against the traditional Lutheran orthodoxy with its strict identification of the eucharistic elements with Christ's body and blood. 'This is the true body of Jesus,' 'This is the true blood of Jesus' were the words of administration in the Danish liturgy then, words which underlined the presence of Christ 'in, with and under' the bread and wine on the altar, to use the classical Lutheran formulae. This seemed to him to involve an imprisoning of the infinite within the finite, too static and exclusive a relation of the heavenly to the earthly. Rather he preferred to see the bread and wine as types and pictures of the heavenly things, a teaching for which, interestingly enough, he sought the support of Clement of Alexandria and Origen as well as of St Paul. And in his earlier teaching they are nothing more than types. But as time went on, and as the influence of Irenaeus grew stronger, he came to appreciate the meaning of the elements in a more positive way. If the whole world is not only a shadow of God's glory, but in some way a sacrament of it, then should not the eucharistic gifts, precisely because parts of that material creation, be fit to partake of the glorious reality which they convey? In particular he began to reflect on the meaning of the chalice, the cup of blessing, which he associated specially with the Holy Spirit. In 1846 he remarks how, on account of the controversies with Rome over the place of the chalice in the sacrament, 'we have almost entirely overlooked its meaning, as the natural image of life and joy, although it is clear enough that it was on this account that the Lord used it in the Supper along with Bread, the natural means of nourishment.'[13] And here again it is the Spirit who brings together earth and heaven, human and divine in a new unity. The chalice of human life and joy is also the chalice of God's love, which unites earth and heaven, and builds up the holy city into a union of love. Leif Kallesen sums up this whole development by saying:

> The basic idea is this, that the miracle of Pentecost becomes present now in and with the living Word which the Holy Spirit speaks in the Supper. Pentecost and Eucharist are bound together reciprocally in such a way that they can represent one another. Pentecost can be an image for the Eucharist, and vice-versa.[14]

Thus in the Eucharist the heavenly and the earthly are fused together in the power of the Spirit, as a sign that the whole earthly creation is called to share in the final transfiguration of all things, when the union of earth and heaven which here we know in faith will be fully and openly revealed. The Agreed Statement on the Eucharist of the present Anglican-Roman Catholic International Commission says:

> In the eucharistic celebration we anticipate the joys of the age to come. By the transforming action of the Spirit of God, earthly bread and wine become the heavenly manna and the new wine, the eschatological banquet for the new man; elements of the first

creation become pledges and first fruits of the new heaven and the new earth.

t is interesting to see an ecumenical group of theologians in the late wentieth century, stressing the same points that Grundtvig was naking almost one hundred and fifty years ago.

Grundtvig himself in a sermon preached on Septuagesima Sunlay, 1834, declares:

so it is just as true that at the Table of the Lord, both bodily and spiritual realities are at work, as the psalmist sings that wine makes glad the heart of man and bread strengthens it, because the bread and wine are not just images of the Lord's body and blood, in which we share spiritually, but are incorporated and taken up into them, by his Word which says, take this and eat it, drink ye all of it. Therefore one of old [i.e. Irenaeus] rightly said that the Lord at the supper took to himself the first creation and confirmed his Word that he had come not to destroy but to fulfil. . . . And now to come back to what is nearest to us today, the vine was undoubtedly one of the trees which God planted in his garden, and to which he gave his blessing to be fruitful and multiply. Yes, it is reasonable to think that it was indeed the tree of life in the midst of the garden, for we are led to conjecture this not only by the wonderful enlivening influence which wine has, when used in moderation even in the fallen condition of this world and our body, but especially because in the Scriptures it is the constant image of God's life-giving Spirit, and is by the Lord himself in his earthly life-time set beside the bread on his table, to merge together (*sammenflyde*) with his blood in the cup of blessing, as a draught of immortality for us both in body and soul.[15]

The care of the vineyard and the tilling of fields
Makes for men upon earth
The bread of life, and the strength of the heart
Above all on the Lord's Table;
For there, in the tent of the Word
Heaven and earth are fused together.
He who takes the Lord

At his word which is spoken there
Rejoices in nectar and ambrosia.

'Wheat corn' and 'vine-stock'
My Lord called himself,
So deliberately leading our mind
To the Bread and Wine on the Table,
Where the heavenly in the Spirit
And the earthly in the hand
Fuse together, basically one
As in the Word, so in the mouth
To the benefit of soul and body.

Wheatcake and the fruit of the vine
Are found on every king's table
But only on the Lord's do they have the strength
which is in God's Spirit and God's Word.
Only there, in the gathering of the Church
does the bread of life become eternal,
Only there does the vine's fruit
have the taste of heaven and divine power
blessedly creating the joy of the heart.[16]

There would be much to be said for making a study of the sacramental thought of Grundtvig in parallel with that of an Orthodox writer
such as Alexander Schmemann, as we see it in his book, *The World as
Sacrament.*

III

From what has been written here it will become clear how vital for
Grundtvig was 'faith in the Holy Spirit as a divine person, Christ's
representative upon earth, the power and life of the Church, its
pastor, teacher and guide'. We can see, too, why he was so disturbed
at the lack of understanding of the person and work of the Spirit in
his day. In 1842 he wrote; in the work from which we have just

quoted: 'From this lack of understanding of the Holy Spirit comes our times' abstract conception of spirit and spiritual reality, and its material concept of freedom and personality, which where they are dominant make any living relationship between heaven and earth, God and man, and thus between Christ and us, evidently impossible.'[17]

One question which immediately comes to mind in considering his position on this subject is 'how strong was the Eastern Orthodox influence on the development of his thought?' It has long been known that in 1837 Grundtvig translated a number of hymns from the Greek of the Byzantine Office Books. Indeed these hymns were the subject of a specialised study some twenty years ago.[18] But only more recently, after the work of Professor Christian Thodberg, has the importance of this episode in Grundtvig's life been more fully realised. Thodberg has shown how deeply the Byzantine hymns affected not only Grundtvig's translations but also some of the finest of his orginal hymns, and how much they inspired his sermons at this time. Thodberg indeed speaks of a 'Greek awakening', as a distinct moment in the development of Grundtvig's thought.[19] There is more that remains to be done here. We know of the influence of Irenaeus in Grundtvig's life. How far did the Greek Fathers in general have an influence on him? How did he arrive at his position on the *filioque*? Was it, as I would suspect, that he reached the conclusion for himself, and then found it confirmed in the Eastern tradition, or was it by a study of the Greek Fathers that he arrived at his own position? It certainly seems that the influence of the Byzantine hymns in 1837 was felt primarily in strengthening and developing lines of thought on which he had already set out, rather than in any radical change of direction.

Whatever the answer to these questions may be, we may safely assert that, on any showing, Grundtvig is one of the great churchmen of nineteenth-century Christendom, and on any definition of theology, other than a narrowly academic one, one of the great theologians of the modern world. That he raises awkward questions for his fellow-Christians of the West is very clear. We are often tempted to say that the comparative neglect of the doctrine of the Holy Spirit in the West is not directly due to the teaching of the *filioque*. Here in our midst is a man of outstanding vision, who rejects the doctrine of the double procession, and at the same time develops a teaching about the person and work of the Spirit of remarkable power and fruitfulness. Was there no connection between these two facts? But Grundtvig may also perhaps raise problems for those of his fellow-Christians who are Eastern Orthodox. How can a man so wholly formed within his own Western tradition, so deeply rooted in the life and worship, the hymns and sacraments of his own Danish Church, approach so closely on many subjects to the teaching of Orthodoxy? Is there a hidden Orthodoxy in the West which reveals itself in unexpected places? To all of us he stands as an ecumenical prophet, as one who encourages us in our search for unity, who assures us of the presence of the risen Christ in the midst of his people through the ever-new action of the Holy Spirit, and who stimulates us to think again of the way in which the whole material creation and all the daily life of men and women in it, is to be caught up into the transfiguring light of God's Kingdom.

NOTES

1. Evagrius Ponticus. *Chapters on Prayer*, No. 60
2. *Den Danske Salmaebog*, 368
3. ibid., 247
4. *For Sammenhaengens Skyld: Ord og motiver i Grundtvigs salmer og praedikener*, ed. Christian Thodberg, Aarhus, 1977 (henceforth cited as *FSS*)
5. Quoted in the article by Morten Mortensen in the *FSS*, 'Hellig-aanden, Guds røst paa jord' (The Holy Spirit, God's Voice on Earth), p. 44
6. ibid., p. 45
7. ibid., p. 49
8. From the article of Erik Krebs Jensen, in the *FSS*, 'Hjertets gud-billedlighed' (The Heart as the Image of God), p. 71
9. See the hymn 'Alle Christne Fødsels-Dag', No. 204 in *Grundtvigs Sang-Vaerk*, 1944 edition, Vol. I
10. Quoted in the article of Christian Højlund in *FSS*, 'Haabets mellemrum' (The Interim of Hope), p. 152
11. ibid., p. 82
12. 'Now as to Grundtvig. At the age of 69 he lost his wife. Within nine months he married again—a widow—on the avowed principle that he was so much in love he could not help it! and *that* for the leader of the movement! I don't want to be hard on the man, but what sort of being must he be?' (Letters of J. M. Neale, edited by his daughter [E. A. Towle], 1910, p. 191)
13. Quoted in the article of Leif Kallesen, in *FSS*, 'Nadverelementerne og Billed-

synet' (The Eucharistic Elements and the Language of Images), p. 196
14. ibid., p. 200
15. Quoted in the article of Lise Brandt Fibiger in *FSS*, 'Grundtvigs vaeksttanke' (Grundtvig's Idea of Growth), p. 245
16. *Sang-Vaerk*, Vol. I., No. 145
17. N. F. S. Grundtvig. *Vaerker i Udvalg*, 1942, Vol. III, p. 430
18. Jórgen Elbek. *Grundtvig og de Graeske Salmer*, 1960
19. Christian Thodberg. *Grundtvigs 'Graeske Vaekkelse'*.

III

THE BALANCE OF TRADITION

6

Trinity and Incarnation in Anglican Tradition

In this chapter we shall attempt to give some account of a central strand in the distinctive theological tradition of the Church of England and to show, if it is possible, certain constant themes and tendencies which have recurred in Anglican theology during the last four centuries.

We shall begin in the present by referring to a book published in 1976 entitled *The Contradiction of Christianity*. It is the work of one of the most creative and profound of Anglican theologians, Canon David Jenkins, who was for some years Director of the Humanum Studies at Geneva for the World Council of Churches, and is now Professor of Theology in the University of Leeds and Director of the William Temple Foundation in Manchester. It is a book, for a large part, concerned with the vital human and social problems which confront mankind at the present time, and with the varying situations which the Christian faith has to meet in different parts of the world. But it contains within itself chapters of a more directly theological nature, luminous pages for instance on the nature of corporate knowledge as the centre of the Church's tradition, or on the restoration of the image and likeness of God in man. It concludes with a chapter, 'The Trinity—love in the end', in which the underlying reasons for the Church's formulation of its belief in God, Father, Son and Holy Spirit are discussed and expounded, and the living significance of that faith affirmed for today. We see the orthodox formulations of the past not as dead or abstract forms of words, but as living powers for the growth of man's life, personal and social, now and in the future. As David Jenkins puts it: 'The Trinity is a symbol for pilgrims who know no limits to their hopes of endurance, discovery and enjoyment.'[1] I refer to this book now at the beginning, and I shall refer to it again at the end, because it seems to me to provide a striking example of the continuing vitality of a tradition which can be traced through the centuries since the breaking of communion between the Church of England and Rome, a tradition which certainly has its roots much earlier than the changes of the sixteenth century.

I

As is well known, the pressures of the State on the Church played a very large part in the English Reformation of the sixteenth century. There was in England at this time no teacher of the power and genius of either Luther or Calvin on the continent of Europe. The particular ability of Thomas Cranmer, the first Reformed Archbishop of Canterbury, was as a liturgist and not as a dogmatic theologian. He gave to our Church its classical formularies of worship in the form of the Book of Common Prayer. The old Latin liturgical tradition was translated into English, the services shortened and adapted so as to allow the people to take an active part in them, and so as to strengthen their scriptural and didactic element. This liturgical tradition, through all its subsequent variations, has remained of primordial importance in forming the Anglican way of living the Christian life and reflecting on the mysteries of the faith. But it was only very gradually in the century following 1558 that a distinctive theological viewpoint emerged within the Church of England. It was not till the middle of the seventeenth century that its outlines had become clearly visible.

Here we have one of the principal reasons for the comparative indistinctness of the Anglican theological position as compared with that of the two main traditions of the continental Reformation. In the case of Luther there grew up from the teaching of the reformer

himself a whole vision of the Christian faith centred upon and controlled by the doctrine of justification by faith alone. In the case of
Calvin, it was the doctrine of the sovereign and predestinating grace
of God which provided the key to an even clearer and more systematic way of expounding the Christian revelation. What theological
principle can we find in the Anglicanism of the period to correspond
to these great and commanding affirmations of the continental
reformers?

To answer this question we shall turn to the two most influential
writers of the classical period of our theological literature, Richard
Hooker (1554–1600) and Bishop Lancelot Andrewes (1555–1626).
But first we must notice a vital point about their theological
method. The Anglican reformers were at one with their continental
contemporaries over against Rome in affirming the supreme authority of Scripture in establishing the faith. 'Are you persuaded that the
Holy Scriptures contain sufficiently all doctrine required of necessity
for eternal salvation through faith in Christ Jesus?' the bishop is
asked at the time of his consecration. But this principle of the
primacy of the Scriptures can be interpreted in many different ways.
As they worked out their own position, the Anglican theologians
came more and more to rely on the concordant testimony of the
teachers of the undivided Church, and in particular on the dogmatic
decisions of the first four General Councils, as providing the way of
approach to the understanding of Scripture. The authority of Scripture was received in and through the witness of Tradition. Nor was
this appeal to the early Church made only in matters of doctrine. In
liturgical and canonical matters it was also significant. In the same
office for the consecration of a bishop, the archbishop begins his
address to the man about to be consecrated, 'Brother, forasmuch as
the Holy Scriptures and the ancient Canons command . . .' thus
linking the authority of the canons with that of Scripture itself. 'As
for my religion', wrote one of the holiest bishops of our Church at
the beginning of the eighteenth century, Thomas Ken, 'I die in the
Holy Catholic and Apostolic faith, professed by the whole Church
before the disunion of East and West, and more particularly I die in
the Communion of the Church of England as it stands distinguished
from all papal and puritan innovations.'

Such a way of approach, which puts great weight on the study of the Fathers, naturally leads towards a theology of a patristic kind. If we ask where we may find the central point of the theology of Richard Hooker, we shall go not to the doctrine of justification, nor to the doctrine of grace, but to the doctrine of the Incarnation of the Word of God. By common consent, the most profound section in the whole of his great work, *On the Laws of Ecclesiastical Polity*, occurs in the fifth book where, turning aside from the details of his controversy with the Puritans about ceremonies and forms of worship, he steps back in order to consider what it is that all the sacraments and rites of the Church signify and perform:

> Sacraments are the powerful instruments of God to eternal life. For as our natural life consisteth in the union of the body with the soul, so our life supernatural in the union of the soul with God. And forasmuch as there is no union of God with man without that mean between both which is both, it seemeth requisite that we first consider how God is in Christ, then how Christ is in us, and how the sacraments do serve to make us partakers of Christ. In other things we may be more brief, but the weight of these requireth largeness.[2]

With these words Hooker introduces his magisterial exposition of Chalcedonian Christology, making it the basis alike of his understanding of the Church and of the sacraments.

If we are looking for the key concepts in Hooker's theological thought, we shall find them in terms such as mutual participation and conjunction, co-inherence and perichoresis. God is in Christ; Christ is in us; we are in him.

> Life, as all other gifts and benefits, groweth originally from the Father and cometh not to us but by the Son, nor by the Son to any of us in particular but through the Spirit. For this cause the Apostle writeth to the church of Corinth, 'The grace of our Lord Jesus Christ, and the love of God, and the fellowship of the Holy Ghost.' Which three Saint Peter comprehendeth in one, 'The participation of the divine Nature'. . . . The Church is in Christ as Eve was in Adam. Yea by grace we are every one of us in Christ

and in his Church, as by nature we are in those our first parents. God made Eve of the rib of Adam. And his Church he formeth out of the very flesh, the very wounded and bleeding side of the Son of man. His body crucified and his blood shed for the life of the world, are the true elements of that heavenly being, which maketh us such as he himself is of whom we come.[3]

It is true that Hooker here avoids the explicit language of *theosis,* (or deification) but it does not escape our attention that when he speaks of Christ 'making us such as he himself is' he affirms the underlying mystery which the word expresses.

It is one of the misfortunes of the Christian West that until the present century, the thought of Maximus the Confessor has been very little known and appreciated. Hooker was a man of amazingly wide erudition, but he can hardly have known the work of the Confessor. Nevertheless I have often thought that there is a certain similarity between them. In both cases one has a theologian with a gift for drawing together and synthesising many varied strands from the previous tradition; a thinker whose work is marked by great balance and judgement. Above all one who does not seek to enhance the glory of God by minimising or denying the goodness of God's creation, but who sets out the way in which the energies of God work in and through all the diversity of the created order. In his own time, Hooker was involved in resisting the tendency in Calvinist theology to exalt God at the expense of man, grace at the expense of nature. He is concerned to defend the true use of reason, the due claims of human institutions and law. But, as a notable Christian writer of our own time, C. S. Lewis, remarks, it would be a great mistake to suppose that this means that there is any tendency towards secularising in him. 'Few model universes are more filled—one might say more drenched—with Deity than his. "All things that are of God [and only sin is not], have God in them and he them in himself likewise"; yet "their substance and his wholly differeth." God is unspeakably transcendent; but also unspeakably immanent.' The whole immensely varied world which God has made is seen in all its multiplicity. The various levels of human life have their own 'laws', their own principles of action. Yet in and through them all the unifying energies of God are at work. 'We meet on all levels the divine wisdom shining through "the beautiful variety of all things in their manifold and yet harmonious dissimilitude".'[4]

The balance and proportion which mark the work of Richard Hooker are to be found in a different form in the writings of his younger contemporary, Bishop Lancelot Andrewes. In his case the heart of his theology is to be found not in his controversial writings, the argument with Bellarmine for instance, but in the great series of sermons preached at Christmas, Easter and Whitsun before the royal court in London, where year by year he expounded the mysteries of Christ's birth, death and resurrection and the coming of the Spirit, with amazing erudition and skill. Here we find the depth and power of his exposition of the Church's faith in Father, Son and Holy Spirit, a faith enriched and enlivened by the wealth of his biblical and patristic knowledge. I intend to examine simply one strand of this fabric, his exposition of the doctrine of *theosis* as the consequence and completion of the doctrine of the Incarnation. I quote from a sermon for Pentecost in which he compares the work of Christ with the work of the Holy Spirit:

> These, if we should compare them, it would not be easy to determine, whether is greater of these two: 1) That of the Prophet, *Filius datus est nobis;* or 2) that of the Apostle, *Spiritus datus est nobis;* the ascending of our flesh, or the descending of His Spirit; *incarnatio Dei,* or *inspiratio hominis;* the mystery of his incarnation, or the mystery of our inspiration. For mysteries they are both, and 'great mysteries of godliness' both; and in both of them 'God is manifested in the flesh'. In the former by the union of His Son; in the latter by the communion of his blessed Spirit. But we will not compare them, they are both above all comparison. Yet this we may safely say of them: without either of them we are not complete, we have not our accomplishment; but by both of them we have, and that fully, even by this day's royal exchange. Whereby, as before he of ours, so now we of his are made partakers. He clothed with our flesh, and we invested with his Spirit. The great promise of the Old Testament accomplished, that he should partake our human nature; and the great and precious promise of the New, that we should be *consortes divinae*

naturae, 'partake his divine nature', both are this day accomplished.[5]

In the case of Lancelot Andrewes we have the benefit of the work of one of the very few Orthodox scholars who have made a detailed study of the Anglican tradition, Nicholas Lossky. In the articles which he has already published, Lossky has contributed much to our understanding of the consistently patristic quality of Andrewes's theology.[6] This particular point illustrates its nature well. There is in Lancelot Andrewes nothing of that reticence towards the doctrine of *theosis* which is to be found in many Western theologians. Rather we find a renewal of the teaching of the Fathers in its fullness, a fullness which includes such themes as the constant progress into God described by St Gregory of Nyssa. In another sermon for Pentecost, Andrewes declares:

> Now to be made partakers of the Spirit, is to be made partakers 'of the divine nature'. That is this day's work. Partakers of the Spirit we are, by receiving grace; which is nothing else but the breath of the Holy Ghost, the Spirit of grace. Grace into the entire substance of the soul, dividing itself into two streams; one goes to the understanding, the gift of faith; the other to the will, the gift of charity, the very bond of perfection. The tongues, to teach us knowledge; the fire, to kindle our affections. The state of grace is the perfection of this life, to grow still from grace to grace, to profit in it. As to go on still forward is the perfection of a traveller, to draw still nearer and nearer to his journey's end.[7]

With this remarkably dynamic definition of the state of grace, as constantly to grow, constantly to go forward, we may leave the work of Lancelot Andrewes, remarking only on its crucial significance in the life of the greatest English poet of our century, T. S. Eliot, who announced his return to the Christian faith in a little volume of essays which he published in 1928 entitled *For Lancelot Andrewes,* and whose understanding of the Christian faith, revealed above all in his *Four Quartets,* is deeply influenced by the vision of the seventeenth-century bishop.

II

The theology of our Church as we find it in the seventeenth century is then a theology of the Incarnation, the Church and the Sacraments. It centres upon the thought of Christ as the head of redeemed humanity, of the Church as his body, of Christians as those who live in him, in the power of the Holy Spirit. During the eighteenth century this tradition grew weaker, though it never altogether disappeared. It was, for instance, expressed by the outstanding representative of our tradition in eighteenth-century America, Dr Samuel Johnson of Connecticut (1696–1772) when he wrote: 'Christ was pleased now to tabernacle in our nature to save mankind, for he took not upon him the nature of angels, but the seed of Abraham, flesh of our flesh and bone of our bone, so as to be truly our head and representative to transact all affairs between God and us which concern our salvation.' The purpose of God's taking flesh was that we might be incorporate in Christ, 'so that by being united to our nature and dwelling in it, he is united to and dwells in us, and we in him. Thus by dwelling in the tabernacle of his Body, he has united himself to and dwells in mankind, especially in all the faithful, who are made members of his Body in Baptism, and are partakers of his blessed body and blood in the holy Eucharist.'[8]

This whole vision of the nature of the Christian life and faith and worship was reaffirmed with great force in the practice of nineteenth-century Anglicanism, in large measure on account of the movement of Church renewal which began in Oxford in 1833. It was a time of much church building, and of great pastoral activity. There was a rediscovery of the riches of the Church's tradition of liturgy and devotion. This practical movement grew out of a renewed faith in the saving reality of the Incarnation, with its double significance 'on the one hand that man's salvation comes from God alone; on the other, that God's saving action really penetrates and transforms man's world and man's life'.[9] The movement itself gave rise to new understandings of the implications of this doctrine, both for the inner life of man, and for life in its social and national dimensions. From the renewal of sacramental life came a new vision of Church's social apostolate, its mission to all humanity. There was implicit in the writings of Hooker and Andrewes a vision of the whole of life as sacramental, and an understanding that this general sacramentality was focussed in the sacraments of the Church— themselves derived from and expressing the mystery of the Incarnate Word, Christ himself, the great sacrament of God's wisdom and God's love. This vision was explicitly drawn out in relation to the new situations of the Church in a world of rapid social change, in the midst of the development of an industrial democracy. In particular the theme of the creation of man in the image of the Triune God was developed with a new urgency; the anthropological consequences of the doctrine of the Trinity became especially important.

We shall look at this theme in the work of theologians whose activity did not lie primarily in the universities, though the solid results of academic theology are presupposed in their teaching, but in the proclamation of the Church's message in the world of their time; in the work of men who may be said to have had a prophetic insight into the needs, personal and social, of Victorian England. In particular we shall look at the work of F. D. Maurice, perhaps the greatest Anglican theologian of the nineteenth century, and of one of his disciples, Thomas Hancock. We shall also consider the teaching of R. M. Benson, the founder of the oldest Anglican community for men, and certainly the outstanding monastic theologian of our Church since the Reformation. We shall notice in all these men a great desire to expound the Church's faith in God the Trinity, not as a matter of mere intellectual assent to a fixed dogmatic formula, but as a living apprehension of the reality of God himself, an apprehension in which we must become aware that it is we who are grasped by God before ever we can, in any sense, grasp him.

'The name of the Trinity', writes F. D. Maurice, 'the Father, the Son and the Holy Ghost is, as the Fathers and Schoolmen said continually, the name of the infinite charity, of the perfect love, the full vision of which is that beatific vision for which saints and angels long even while they dwell in it.' To speak of God as Trinity is, for Maurice, to give substance to our faith that God is love. This is not a faith which Maurice accepted passively; it was one which he had gained through personal travail. His father was a Unitarian minister, and as a young man Maurice passed through a period of agnosticism. It was only in adult life that he was baptised into the Name

of the Father, the Son and the Holy Spirit. And this is a faith which
for him not only declares the true nature of God; it also declares the
true nature and calling of man. For all men are to be baptised into
this Name, which is to unite the nations into one, 'by which men
may be raised to the freedom and righteousness and fellowship for
which they were created'. As Bishop Michael Ramsey comments in
his valuable study of Maurice's teaching: 'Since the Triune God is
the creator of the human race, the likeness of his eternal charity
dwells in the human race, and the Trinity in Unity is the source of
human fellowship in those who repent of their self-centred isolation
and discover the true principal of their being.'[10]

This thought is given expression in a remarkable sermon of
Thomas Hancock preached in 1869, with the title 'The Fellowship
in God the Source of Humanity's Fellowship with God', the whole
of which constitutes a powerful affirmation of faith in the living God
of Scripture and Tradition:

> The human person through whom we have access to God is, the
> faith declares, God the Son. There is no certainty that God is the
> Father unless it be true that he has and ever has had, a co-eternal
> Son . . . St Hilary boldly said: 'We could not preach one God to
> men, if we had to preach a lonely God.' God is not merely *One*,
> not a mere unity, but he is the one *God*, that is, the one who is
> good, the one who includes in his perfect unity all possible
> good. . . . The Divine Unity into whose Name the Son through
> whom we have access to that Unity commands us to baptise all
> nations and every creature, is a Divine Unity; he is not a Divine
> solitariness, a Divine egotism . . . We ourselves deteriorate by
> the absence of fellowship, and we lose the power of drawing to us
> the faith and love and worship of others. God's revelation of
> himself to his human creatures as the Trinity in Unity—as
> Father, Son and Holy Ghost, one God—has drawn forth from
> men of all ages and places, of all degrees of culture and ignorance,
> the most wonderful joy, hope, faith and love. A man is at his
> highest, he is most perfectly a man, he is most godly, when he is
> living not as a mere unit, but as the fellow of a unity, as a
> kinsman in the family, as a citizen in the state, as a catholic in the
> Church, as a man in the human-kind. . . . He who made us is not

a cold, hard, lonely, self-amusing Mechanician, caring little what becomes of his experiments. In his being subsists the perfect Fellowship, the perfect Communion of which we have some imperfect shadow in our being, and for whose reproduction in us and our kind we crave with so insatiable a hunger.[11]

At every point Hancock, like his teacher Maurice, looks beyond the Church to the whole of humanity and the whole creation. He does this not because he regards the Church as of little importance, but because he believes that he who is the head of the Church is also, in some sense, the head of all humanity, the one in whom all men are to find their true destiny and calling.

If we enter ever so little into the contemplation of the depths of the Catholic Faith—that is, the faith for all human kind and for every creature—we shall find it impossible to separate the unity of the Church from the unity of humanity; we shall find it impossible to separate the unity of humanity from the unity of God in Trinity. If we do not see that man's unity is in God, and that we can each enter into it in him, we shall seek it as the first violaters of the unity of mankind sought it, in some Tower of Babel—some colossal manufacture of human hands and brains.[12]

Here is a vision of the Church as the representative of all mankind gathered together in the power of the Spirit, called to participate in the very life of the Triune God. It was this understanding of things which forced Maurice himself, and all those whom he influenced, to look beyond the frontiers of the Church, to be concerned for the whole of human life. From the doctrines of the Incarnation and the Trinity, understood not as dead or abstract formulae, but as living and life-giving affirmations of faith and hope, they drew a whole programme of social action. Hancock in his own time was a prophetic voice, too little heeded. His outspoken denunciation of social and economic evils, taken together with the angularity of his character, prevented him from reaching a prominent position in the Church. He remained an assistant priest with no public status and very little recognition, one who was identified to an unusual degree with the hopes and aspirations of the industrial workers. But his theological

vision was by no means his alone. He shared it with a whole group of
men who had been inspired by the thought of F. D. Maurice. We
find it again in a very different representative of the priesthood of the
Church of England in the nineteenth century, Father R. M. Benson,
the Superior and Founder of the Society of St John the Evangelist at
Cowley in Oxford.

With Father Benson we face the mystery and the miracle of the
restoration of spiritual gifts which had for long been neglected or
ignored. For more than three hundred years there had been no
monastic communities in the Church of England; now unexpectedly
in the middle of the nineteenth century the gift of monastic life and
monastic prayer was renewed. And with the gift of prayer and life
there went, in the case of Benson, a gift of theology, understood
much more in the sense in which the Fathers use that term than in
the way in which it has commonly been used in the West in recent
centuries. 'The use of the intellect is', he writes, 'that by knowing
the things of God we may attain to the experimental knowledge of
God's love. Otherwise our learning is only like a staircase leading to
the top of a ruined tower.' And again: 'It is not enough for us to
know what was fixed as the orthodox expression: we must have our
minds trained affectionately in the orthodox consciousness, which is
deeper and larger than the expression . . . by intellectual study we
must gather up the teaching of past ages in the fullness of its scope.
We have not to maintain truth, but to live in the truth so that it
may maintain us.'[13]

Like F. D. Maurice, but I believe quite independently of him, the
distinction between person and individual became for Father Benson
of vital importance. When we speak of the individual we speak of
man in his isolation, in his separateness, of man as competitor.
When we speak of the person we speak of man in relationship, in
communion, man as co-worker. If the life of the whole Church is in
some sense a reflection or icon of the mystery of the Triune love,
then the life of the community is to be so in a special way, for it is
the purpose of the community 'to gather up and, as it were, focus
the love which ought to animate the whole body of the Church
Catholic.' We can see something of the way in which Benson taught
if we consider this extract from an instruction given to his brethren
in the first years of the community's life. We see how his teaching

was at once very practical and deeply theological.

> Thy whole life must be a relative life. The moment thou art
> imprisoned in thine own self-consciousness, in thine own separate
> individuality, in the selfishness of thine own separated existence,
> thou committest a worse suicide than taking the life of thy body.
> Thou destroyest the very life of thy person. Thy person is a
> relative being and thou hast no existence save when thou actest
> for others. Man is created to be a social being. And as the Three
> Divine Persons have no life whatsoever except in this relativity of
> action, so we have no life whatsoever except in relative action
> towards others ... It is the law of our nature that our life is
> personal, relative, communicating all that it has. It is the law
> under which the Christian Church, the Body of Christ, is consti-
> tuted. 'They had all things in common.' Property belongs to the
> dead world—community is the life of God.[14]

Remarkable words to come from the heart of nineteenth-century
England. As St Antony says, 'Your brother is your life.'

But, of course, it is not only in inter-personal relations that we
come to know God. There is an inner journey of love and knowledge
which leads us towards an ever-increasing entry into 'the dwelling
places of the Three in One'. So it is not surprising that the doctrine
of *theosis* is developed by Father Benson with remarkable emphasis.
As a recent study of his Trinitarian theology concludes:

> Christian life, fully realised and lived, is nothing less than par-
> ticipation in the Divine life—it is *theosis,* deification. . . . Con-
> stantly he uses the word 'deific' in its strict and full sense. He
> repeats the thought that it is 'into the Divine Life that we are
> gathered by our regeneration'; that we are 'made partakers of the
> Divine Nature', that 'we are called to participate in the uncreated
> energy of God'. His critique of nineteenth-century Christendom
> implies that the capacity to live the gospel authentically is
> entirely dependent on a vision of the unlimited resources of
> energy and love to which, in this deified relationship, the believer
> has access. The Christian life can be lived only when the Triune
> Life of God is 'felt as a power'.[15]

In the conjunction of pure theology with compassionate love for all men, there is an interesting parallel with St Calinic of Cernica, a contemporary of Father Benson and the most recently canonised saint of Romania. Father Benson, however, has not been widely read and it is only now, after almost a century, that the true importance of his theology, to which Bishop Ramsey pointed more than thirty years ago, is beginning to be understood, and the relevance of his teaching to the twentieth century better appreciated.

III

We are brought back irresistibly to the witness of the contemporary theologian with whom we began. David Jenkins also has a critique of our twentieth-century Christendom, a Christendom in which our actions all too often give the lie to things which we affirm in our faith, so that orthodoxy is not always matched by orthopraxy or, to put it more simply, so that right thought is not always supported by right action. For David Jenkins, as for Benson, it is a failure of vision which lies at the root of our problems, a failure of vision 'of the unlimited resources of energy and love to which the believer has access, when the Triune Life of God is felt as power'. Of course, Jenkins is facing a different set of problems from those which Father Benson faced a hundred years ago. The terms which he uses are often different. It is a testimony to the living nature of the tradition which he expresses that this should be so. To be true to the tradition is not primarily a question of repeating formulae. It is to live in communion with our fathers in the faith, sharing with them one vision and one life, the life which comes from God. It is to grow in the orthodox consciousness, which is deeper and larger than the orthodox expression. Not surprisingly for one who has worked and thought at the centre of the World Council of Churches, Jenkins is vividly aware of the many changes which are taking place in our world, changes at a spiritual level as well as at a social one: the shift of influence and initiative from Europe and North America to the countries of the Third World, the sudden enhancement of the position of women in society, the problems and the opportunities inherent in the process of rapid social change, the threat of violence, and the threat of war in our world situation.

As a theologian Jenkins is concerned to look in and through particular issues to the underlying features of the human situation, to seek for a renewal of vision of what it is to be man. He is sharply critical of the habit, particularly strong in the English-speaking countries, of looking only for 'pragmatic' solutions.

> If we insist on being, as we call it, 'pragmatic' (or 'matter-of-fact') and refuse deeper reflection, disturbance or exploration, then we are bound to be treating human beings as simply 'things', that is, as nothing but an interesting collection of the *pragmata* from which the adjective 'pragmatic' derives. But human beings are not things, they are persons. And in the Christian vision and understanding they are not even just historical persons (although they are at least that), they are potentially eternal persons.[16]

What is the nature of this vision? It is something very different from what we should call a 'mere theory', an intellectual abstraction with no necessary connection with life and experience. Rather it is something very close to the *theoria* of the Greek Fathers:

> . . . a practical and practising insight into a living mystery. For the word *theoria* was used, and needs to be revived, to refer to a spiritual capacity to develop insight into the vision and action of God, both beyond all things and through all things. This capacity is developed and deepened by the grace of God received through fellowship and the discipline of prayer, worship and a sustained pursuit of Christian discipleship in all things. Indeed, the spiritual capacity to see into and respond to the very heart and energy of things is the expression and experience of being in the image of God. It is because men and women are created by God in the image of God that they have the capacity to see and respond to him and to his energetic activities and possibilities in one another, in themselves and in all things.[17]

This consideration of man as created in God's image necessarily leads us to further reflection on the anthropological significance of the doctrine of the Trinity. But here an important point of terminology must be noted. Just as Christian *theoria* is far from being mere theory, so Christian doctrine is far from being merely intellectual and verbal. Jenkins prefers to speak of teaching about the Trinity as a symbol or icon:

> It has been the subject of much doctrinal discussion and reflects the insights gained and clarified in those discussions. But it operates as an articulated picture, with a worked out, recognised and traditional pattern which continues in use as a focus for and provocation of experience. The shape and pattern of this icon was worked out to present and represent a living possibility. This was (and is) glimpsed in images, words and actions. The whole process is kept alive by the activity the symbol reflects. Thus 'the Trinity' stands, not for a doctrine, but for a way of life which is related to God's life.[18]

Thus to speak of the Holy Trinity is to speak of the immediacy and depth of the Church's apprehension of God as being at once immanent and transcendent. It is to speak of the particularity of his action in the flesh and blood of Jesus of Nazareth, and at the same time to affirm the universality of his action at all times and in all places. It speaks first

> of the over-ruling energy and presence of the transcendent God who is both the God of Israel and the God of the whole earth ... secondly, of the historic energy and activity of Jesus, who he was, what he did and what was undergone by him and revealed through him in the episode of the cross and. resurrection ... thirdly, of the immanent activity of the Spirit continuing the story, developing the story, maintaining the knowledge of the story in actual communities and relating the implications of the story to living in touch with concrete realities.[18]

And a little further on Jenkins continues:

> Thus the symbol of the Trinity insists on and lays claim to a unique way of holding together transcendence and immanence,

eternity and history, God and human beings. This, it proclaims, is the necessary and legitimate interpretation of the experienced and perceived story of God, Jesus and the Spirit, and of the story which therefore follows about God, men and the world. The dependent and temporary realities of nature and history, and of the conditions of human living within them, are in no way diminished as to their autonomy, authenticity and significance by the commitment of God to them and the involvement of God in them. At the same time God is neither defined nor limited by his unlimited involvement and his unambiguous commitment. He is Transcendence known to us as Transcendence in the midst.[20]

This is why in this vision of the Trinity we see the structure of supreme love, the affirmation of the reality of the presence of God's love in us and with us, that love which raises the dead and calls the things that are not into being and into life, that love which opens to men and women in all the limitations and fragility of their human existence, the infinite possibilities of the life and activity of God. 'Therefore it is clear that although God can be God without man and that God *is* God without man, none the less God *will not* be God without man. He does not need us. He loves us.'[21]

While it is certainly true that a single book by a single writer can hardly be taken to sum up the teaching of a whole theological tradition, it cannot be denied that this particular work, with its combination of a profound Chalcedonian orthodoxy in its exposition of the doctrines of the Incarnation and the Trinity, together with sensitive and perceptive awareness of the realities, spiritual and social, of our own day, represents in a remarkable way the latest growth of that tradition whose development we have sought to trace in this study. Taken together with Jenkins's earlier work, *The Glory of Man,* it offers us a striking testimony to the vitality of a theological position too often ignored in Western ecumenical debate.

IV

What the importance of this theological tradition for the Eastern

Orthodox will finally be is, of course, for the Orthodox themselves to say. They may well be inclined to ask how far it is possible to consider the theological position outlined here to be representative of Anglicanism as a whole when other writers could have been cited of different viewpoints who would also claim to speak on behalf of the Anglican Communion. The question is a real one. It is true that since the sixteenth century the Anglican tradition has contained within itself different schools of thought. Nevertheless, the Christological and Trinitarian emphases which characterise the writers we have quoted are, I believe, typical of that way of thought and teaching which is most central, most permanent and most significant in the history of our Church. On any showing, Hooker, Andrewes and Maurice would be acknowledged as three outstanding spokesmen of our position. That there are points of convergence between the position indicated here and the Orthodox tradition would seem sufficiently clear. How significant these similarities are is perhaps not yet wholly evident. For myself I must say that the parallels between the writers I have cited and representative Orthodox scholars seem very striking. In particular there are remarkable parallels with much that has been written in the renewal of Romanian Orthodox theology in the last thirty years, and one is led to wonder whether, in addition to the general affinity of Anglican with Orthodox, there is a specific relationship between English and Romanian theology due in part to the mediating positions held by these two nations. These are questions which deserve to be further investigated. One point which it is interesting to note is that while all the authors quoted in this paper were familiar with the writings of the Fathers, at least with those of the first five centuries, none except David Jenkins had any direct theological contact with their Eastern Orthodox contemporaries. If there are real points of agreement they have been reached through fidelity to common origins, not through any direct influence or imitation.

From the Anglican side I am convinced that the fuller and more conscious recognition of our relationship to Orthodoxy is of crucial importance for the future of our tradition. The encounter with Orthodoxy can provide us with a key which enables us to understand the development of that tradition in a new and more coherent way. The *via media* which our Church has always sought to preserve since the break with Rome is no longer seen as a mere compromise, but as an attempt to witness in the West to a fullness and a balance of the faith which Orthodoxy has always preserved in the East. What I should like to ask my Orthodox colleagues is whether the encounter with Anglicanism, not only in its contemporary representatives but in its outstanding spokesmen during the last four centuries, may not provide them with a clue to finding new ways to expound and live their faith in a world which has been so largely shaped by ideas and forces coming from the West. How far has it been given to the Churches of the Anglican Communion to prepare a place in the West where the faith and life of Orthodoxy may find its own roots, its hitherto unacknowledged Western tradition? In a world which has suddenly become one, not only at an economic but also at a spiritual level, the old rigid distinctions of East and West are increasingly ceasing to have meaning. It is in a new realisation of the unity of all mankind in the providence and love of the Triune God, Father, Son and Holy Spirit, that we are being called together at the present time.

NOTES

1. David Jenkins. *The Contradiction of Christianity*, 1976, p. 145
2. Richard Hooker. *The Laws of Ecclesiastical Polity*, ed. John Keble, 1836, Book V, ch. 1.3, p. 218
3. ibid., V, ch. lvi. 7, p. 249
4. C. S. Lewis. *English Literature in the Sixteenth Century*, 1954, pp. 459–61
5. Lancelot Andrewes. *Complete Works*, Library of Anglo-Catholic Theology, 11 Vols 1841–54, Vol. III, pp. 108–9
6. Nicholas Lossky. *Sobomost*, Series 6, No. 2, pp. 78–89
7. Andrewes, *op, cit., p.* 367
8. Louis Weil.'Worship and Sacraments in the Teaching of Samuel Johnson of Connecticut'. Unpublished doctoral thesis at the Institut Catholique in Paris, 1972, pp. 146–7
9. E. R. Fairweather (ed.). *The Oxford Movement*, 1964, p. 11
10. A. M. Ramsey. *F. D. Maurice and the Conflicts of Modern Theology*, 1951, pp. 54–5
11. Quoted in A. M. Allchin, *The Spirit and the Word: Two Studies in Nineteenth-century Anglican Theology*, 1963, pp. 55–7
12. ibid., p. 60
13. R. M. Benson. *Followers of the Lamb*, 1905, pp. 10–11
14. From the MS volume of the *Retreat of July 1874*, at Cowley

15. See the article by Martin Smith, SSJE in *Christian*, Vol. 4, No. 1, Epiphany 1977, p. 24
16. David Jenkins. *The Contradiction of Christianity* (see note 1), p. 99
17. ibid., p. 100
18. ibid., p. 143
19. ibid., p. 150
20. ibid., p. 157
21. ibid.

7

The Book of Common Prayer and The Continuity of Tradition

I

The title of this chapter conceals a certain ambiguity. It would be possible to speak of the Book of Common Prayer and the continuity of tradition within the Anglican Communion during the last four centuries, which the book has done so much to maintain. Such a subject would in itself be worth while, and we shall not altogether neglect it. But it is also possible to understand the topic in a wider and more general way. This would allow us to consider the history of Anglican worship, not just in itself, but in relation to that older and larger tradition of prayer and praise, which has its roots in the Old Testament, which flowers throughout the Christian centuries and of which the Anglican tradition forms only one small part. It is primarily in this way that we shall consider our subject here, seeking to see it in relation to a concern for the continuity of the Christian tradition of common prayer and praise taken as a whole.

To view the matter in this way is immediately to recognise that the Book of Common Prayer is at once a symbol of continuity and discontinuity. On the one side it has provided the means by which the liturgical tradition of the pre-Reformation Church has been continued, albeit in a modified form, in the worship of Anglicans and of many Methodists. One of the most remarkable characteristics of the Book is its ecumenical quality. Since 1559, it has contained no denunciations or anathemas. It prays always 'for the whole state of Christ's Church', 'for all who profess and call themselves Christians', 'for the good estate of the Catholic Church', and only for the Church of England, or any other particular Church province, as contained within that greater whole. Its very title page declares that it is a book containing the rites and sacraments *of the Church,* 'according to the use of the Church of England', thereby at the outset appealing to the whole Christian tradition. On the other side, it has been, together with the Thirty-nine Articles, the distinctive formulary by which the Anglican tradition has marked itself off from Rome on the one side, and from the principal strands of English-speaking Protestantism on the other. Indeed the vigorous Puritan criticism of the book as maintaining far too much of the pre-Reformation tradition, was already making this double, and perhaps paradoxical, character evident within a generation of the final break with Rome. The book is a vehicle of continuity produced in a moment of sharp discontinuity.

And here we find the particular fascination of this topic for our own day. We, too, live in a moment in which discontinuity is at least as evident as continuity in the patterns of worship of Western Christendom. Within the last twenty-five years the liturgy of the Roman Catholic Church, by far the largest and most influential part of our Western Christian family, has undergone changes in some ways as radical and rapid as those which occurred in the Reformation Churches during the sixteenth century. None of our Reformation traditions has been altogether unaffected by these moves. Anglicans have been particularly influenced by this revolution, which, quite incidentally to its main purpose, has meant that we no longer have a monopoly of a fixed vernacular liturgy. What distinguished us from Roman Catholics now unites us with them.

These changes which have occurred so suddenly in Rome, have had their more gradual counterparts with us. The comparative uniformity of the Prayer Book tradition has given place to a unity in diversity which becomes clearly evident whenever Anglicans of different Church provinces gather together, as for instance at the Lambeth Conference of 1978, where day by day the bishops of the various Churches celebrated their variously reformed and renewed liturgies. Everywhere in the Anglican Communion revised prayer books are appearing. In the United States of America, the Episcopal Church has one of the finest of these revised books, the work of the most distinguished liturgical commission to be found in the Anglican Communion. But of course in all Christian traditions of the West this is a moment of liturgical reform and renewal. There are common questions which confront us all. Shall we be able to maintain a vital thread of continuity through the discontinuities of our time? Is there an underlying unity of tradition which is compatible with a diversity of outward expression? Is this unity of tradition, in fact a living thing which carries within itself possibilities of adaptation and development?

And there is more at stake here than the question of the revision of liturgical forms, of the way for instance in which, in our time, Churches with fixed liturgies have found it necessary to allow for greater flexibility and variation within their structures, and Churches without fixed liturgies have found that the production of at least outline forms of worship plays a vital part in the renewal of the worshipping life of their congregations. More fundamental questions are being raised about the possibility of any real continuity with the Christian way of prayer and worship, as it has been known in the past. In such a situation we certainly need a theological as well as a purely historical approach to the study of liturgy.

Perhaps I may suggest what I have in mind by recounting a small but fairly typical incident. Going into Canterbury Cathedral for Evensong one day I fell into conversation with an impressively bearded figure who told me that he was a Methodist minister from a middle-western State, but that he had spent the last two years in India learning the arts of meditation from a number of Tibetan masters. It had begun to strike him that perhaps there was something to be explored in this area in his own Christian tradition. He seemed surprised when I suggested that he might do worse than to start with the hymns of Charles Wesley. We have lived and are living through a time when many within the Churches, theologians and Church leaders among them, have doubted whether it is possible to maintain the Christian tradition of public prayer and inner spiritual discipline, in any way which has meaning or is relevant. These doubts have been expressed in words by some theologians. They are, I am afraid, often expressed more powerfully and generally by the ways in which we order our Church life; by the low priorities we give to the practice and study of common prayer and personal meditation and contemplation in the allocation of our time and energy. It is not surprising that, in the face of this atrophy of the Church's tradition of prayer and praise, people, especially young people, have been led to look elsewhere, have turned to other religions, which seem to offer a much more systematic approach to the experience and knowledge of the divine, that some of those in search of God have turned their back, at least for a time, on the Christian tradition. We have even seen the surprising phenomenon of the monastic life, being re-invented not so much within the Churches, as around and beyond them.

II

At such a moment, is it possible that a structure like the Book of Common Prayer, perhaps the primary liturgical text of our English-speaking Christianity, can reveal an unlooked-for potential of life and renewal? Can it convey at least a certain potentiality of inner experience and understanding, of an experimental grasp of the great mysteries of Christian faith? Have these texts in the past conveyed, at least implicitly, a knowledge and a love which seem largely lost to us? Are they capable of coming to life in our own time, of surprising us by their vitality, somewhat in the way in which they did in England and America in the middle of the nineteenth century, when the Eucharistic content of the Prayer Book, which for more than a century had been seriously obscured, suddenly re-asserted itself in the wake of the Oxford Movement? In the eighteenth century it was rare indeed to find clergymen like John and Charles Wesley who celebrated the Holy Communion with the frequency required by the Prayer Book. How far will the Prayer Book need to be supplemented and enriched from other strands in the Christian tradition of worship, Eastern as well as Western, if it is to respond to the needs of our own ecumenical century?

The asking of these larger questions has been prompted by a remarkable study of the thought of the greatest of Anglican theologians, completed in 1977 by a French scholar Olivier Loyer, who teaches in the University of Paris.[1] This work, *The Anglicanism of Richard Hooker, an Essay on his philosophical, political and theological Thought*, remains unfortunately untranslated and as yet unpublished, but it stimulates much reflection in an Anglican on the nature and development of the tradition by which he lives, and not least on the significance of the Prayer Book within it. The centrality of the Book of Common Prayer in Anglicanism is due in the first place to the liturgical genius of Archbishop Thomas Cranmer. But it is due in the second place to the theological genius of Richard Hooker. We have not sufficiently reflected on the fact that the greatest and most influential theological work to have been produced in our tradition since the Reformation, should have been so deeply concerned with the defence of the Church's tradition of prayer and worship, and with the exposition of its inner meaning and coherence. It is in the conjunction of Thomas Cranmer and Richard Hooker that we find the roots of the continuing Anglican concern with prayer and liturgy. In Richard Hooker we recognise a theology which reflects the scope and balance of the liturgy and itself enriches our understanding of it. It is a theology of prayer and sacrament founded in the doctrine of the Incarnation, and in a profound meditation on the co-inherence of God and man in Christ and in the Holy Spirit. It is a meditation which leads us into the very heart of the Christian mystery, and which may be seen to spring up from the words which Cranmer puts into the mouth of the celebrant as he approaches the central point in the Eucharist, the prayer that 'we may evermore dwell in him an he in us'. We shall be seeking then to look at these innermost meanings and realities which the Prayer Book enshrines, rather than at the detail of its outward structure, to consider those inner principles which in large measure it shares with all major liturgical traditions and which provide the unity and coherence underlying its present variety of form.

It would, however, be a complete misunderstanding, indeed a betrayal of the tradition of the Prayer Book, to suggest that inner meaning and reality could be divorced from outward and historical form. We may distinguish them, but we must not separate them. For one of the primary elements which the tradition contains is the insistence on the conjunction of outward sign and inward meaning, bodily gesture and spiritual significance. The sacramental principle was something bitterly contested in the sixteenth and seventeenth centuries. It was one of the points particularly stressed by one of the few outstanding Anglican scholars of eighteenth-century America, Samuel Johnson of Connecticut. In our own time, in which we have become newly aware of the symbolic nature of things, it gains a new and surprising importance. Let us, therefore, look first at some of the formal aspects of the Book, and at the way in which they have given structure to Anglican faith and worship through the past four centuries.

The Prayer Book is in itself a masterpiece of comprehensiveness, using that word in its original meaning of drawing together, comprehending much in a small space. It is, as it says, a Book of *Common* Prayer, for the use of the whole people of God, intended to let all, clergy and laity together, exercise the royal priesthood entrusted to them. At every turn it presupposes the centrality of the Scriptures in Christian faith and worship; it is full of Biblical material. At the same time it contains all that is necessary for the weekly celebration of the Eucharist, and it suggests that, at least at the great feasts of Christmas, Easter and Whitsun, the Eucharist will be celebrated daily. In the festivals of the Church's year it manifests the outline of the Church's faith, and in the commemoration of the saints reminds us of what Christ has done in those who are his members. It contains on either side of this Eucharistic section, the means of continuing the tradition of the daily praise of God, the *laus perennis,* in the daily Offices of morning and evening prayer, and in the directions for the recitation of the Psalter. Here is an element in the tradition which is surely no less important than the Eucharistic strand which it complements and sustains. It has received and continues to receive a particular emphasis in the daily choral worship of the English cathedrals. The book also contains the forms which convey the Christian from his new birth in Baptism through health and sickness to the moment of burial. It is a personal book no less than a communal one. Finally it provides for all to see the forms by which the Church's traditional ministries of bishop, priest and deacon are to be retained and carried forward. Of the five lesser rites known as sacraments in the Western Church, four, confirmation, marriage, confession and ordination are provided in the Book of Common Prayer. It is small wonder that it has itself revealed a converting power, holding out to men and women a vision of the wholeness of the life of the believer within the greater wholeness of the communion of all who profess and call themselves Christians.

But while we recognise the greatness and the power of Cranmer's vision and achievement as expressed in the Prayer Book, we must be careful not to make an idol of it. The Prayer Book has always been at the centre of the Anglican tradition of worship. It has never been the whole of it. Already in the sixteenth century, the need for metrical versions of the Psalms had made itself felt. More recently there has been a great development of hymnody to supplement the somewhat didactic tone of its rites, and to give the affective element in worship more scope. Again within the first century of the Prayer Book's history occasions occurred for which it did not provide. There were national triumphs and disasters to be commemorated, kings and queens to be crowned, church buildings to be consecrated. The book was supplemented in various ways, in part by adaptations of material from the earlier tradition of East and West. Two of the greatest bishops of the seventeenth century, Lancelot Andrewes of Winchester in his *Preces Privatae,* and John Cosin of Durham in his *Collection of Private Devotions* provided for the ordinary members of the Church of England access to areas of the liturgical tradition of the undivided Church only partially represented in the Prayer Book. Lancelot Andrewes drew much on the tradition of the Christian East. Cosin familiarised Anglicans with the lesser offices of the Western monastic tradition. Both works underlined the way in which the Common Prayer of the Church needs to overflow into the devotions of families and individuals and to be supported by the practice of constant prayer outside the liturgy.

Thus it is that within Great Britain itself the tradition was never quite so monolithic or so monoglot as has commonly been believed. A Latin translation of the Prayer Book was prepared for use in the Universities of Oxford and Cambridge already in 1560. It contains small but significant variations from the English text. Within the first half of the reign of Elizabeth I, the Prayer Book no less than the Bible was translated into Welsh. The result was that the splendid prose style of the Renaissance Welsh scholars was heard Sunday by Sunday in the parish churches throughout Wales. The Bible was not

only studied, it was read aloud and sung. The older language of
Britain was prevented from being fragmented into a number of
dispersed dialects. The way was prepared for the doctrinal strength
and coherence of the Welsh Methodist revival. We may think in
particular of the stress on the wonder of the Incarnation, God in man
and man in God, to be found alike in the hymns of Williams
Pantycelyn and Ann Griffiths. In Scotland there was a different
story. In the first half of the seventeenth century, the bishops there
produced a revised form of the Eucharistic prayer, thereby correcting
one of the most idiosyncratic of all the innovations of Cranmer.
Rejected in its own time, this fuller form of the prayer was taken up
again and amplified in the years of persecution in the eighteenth
century. With Samuel Seabury it crossed the Atlantic and placed the
invocation of the Holy Spirit at the heart of the sacramental life of
the Episcopal Church. If, as has recently been declared, 'the Church
is that Community which lives by continually invoking the Holy
Spirit,'[2] then this is a matter of no little significance in the history
of Anglicanism in North America. What we see, therefore, is that
from the beginning there was a capacity for translation, for adaptation and development in the Prayer Book tradition which has not
been sufficiently noted. There was also, as is particularly clear in the
works of Cosin and Andrewes, a willingness to go to the sources, an
appeal to the wider tradition of the Church to enrich and enlarge the
provision contained within the book. The adaptations and enrich-
ments of more recent years, for instance in the re-introduction of the
traditional ceremonies for Holy Week and Easter, or the recovery of
the rite for the anointing of the sick, have their precedents in the
sixteenth and seventeenth centuries.

III

We have spoken earlier of the possibility that in our own day this
tradition might be capable of revealing unexpected powers of adaptation, and of responding in unlikely ways to the unprecedented
needs of our own time. What those needs are, is a question to which
very many answers are possible. But I suppose that it would be

widely agreed that the developments of the last ten years, both in North America and Western Europe, have suggested that we are faced with an undeniable spiritual hunger, a renewed thirst for the experienced knowledge and love of God. We observe a desire to rediscover suppressed or neglected aspects of man's being, his search for the transcendent, his capacity for delight and wonder, for a non-exploitative attitude towards the world around. We see a desire to re-integrate the body into the totality of life, not least the life of prayer and worship. The problems of ecology, the rediscovery of the sacredness of the material world, the nature of spiritual, indeed mystical, experience, these are questions which are alive now in a way in which they were not ten or fifteen years ago.

We have said already that the Prayer Book enshrines a sacramental principle, the possibility of seeing the 'World as Sacrament', to borrow a phrase from a distinguished American Orthodox theologian.[3] This sacramental principle is, I believe, of vital importance for our time. It is, as John Keble remarks in his introduction to his edition of Hooker's works, one of the basic themes in the theology of Richard Hooker, a principle which he drew not only from his own experience of worship but from his study of the witness of the early Church.

> The primitive apostolical men, being daily and hourly accustomed to sacrifice and dedicate to God even ordinary things, by mixing them up with Christian and heavenly associations, might well consider everything whatever as capable of becoming ... a means of grace, a pledge and token of Almighty presence and favour ... God omnipresent was so much in their thoughts, that what to others would have been mere symbols, were to them designed expressions of his Truth, providential intimations of his Will. In this sense, the whole world, to them, was full of sacraments.[4]

It is this understanding of the nature of the material world which informs Hooker's defence of the outward and visible aspects of the Church's worship, for instance his justification of the practice of dedicating particular places and particular times to the service of God. It is because God is present in all times and all places that he can make himself known in particular buildings, and in particular days and commemorations which are made over to him. 'For as God by being everywhere yet doth not give unto all places one and the same degree of godliness, so neither one and the same dignity to all times by working in all.'[5] God, in whom all things exist, yet makes himself known amongst men. The principle of the Incarnation works itself out in many ways. The kingdom of God is amongst us and within us and, taking up an understanding of the Church's worship particularly powerful in the Eastern Christian tradition, Hooker sees in the assembly of the Church at prayer the presence of heaven on earth, the anticipation of the joy of the kingdom.

Hence we find in his writings, as we do in the preaching of some of the outstanding figures of the seventeenth century, pre-eminently Lancelot Andrewes, but also less well-known men like Mark Frank, a wonderful sense of the richness of liturgical time, of the moment of worship as one in which the past is gathered up, re-membered, the future fulfilment anticipated and made known, in a moment which is one of an intensity of presence. In the power of the Spirit, the risen Christ is made known in our midst; the Father's love is proclaimed in word and deed. It is this awareness of the presence of God in the Church's worship, which gives to the liturgy its quality of joy, a joy which the world can neither give nor take away, a joy in which man finds the fulfilment of his being. It is this which gives rise to the outward splendour of the Church's worship, in music, building and ritual action. It is this which is the motive power behind the Christian transformation of the world and of human relationships within it. For while, in Hooker's view, *Rest* and *Praise* are two of the characteristics of the Church's festivals, so no less is *Bounty,* overflowing generosity. Let us hear him on this subject:

The joy that setteth aside labour disperseth those things which labour gathereth. For gladness doth always arise from a kind of fruition and happiness, which happiness banisheth the cogitation of all want, it needeth nothing but only the bestowing of that it hath, inasmuch as the greatest felicity that felicity hath is to spread and enlarge itself. It cometh hereby to pass that the first effect of joyfulness is to rest, because it seeketh no more, the next because it aboundeth, to give. The root of both is the glorious presence of that joy of mind, which riseth from the manifold considerations of God's unspeakable mercy, into which considerations we are led by occasion of sacred times.[6]

Through the presence of eternity in time, the active calling to mind of the liberating, pardoning acts of God, man is made free, his life made full of meaning and direction. Time itself is no longer squeezed out of shape by the constant pressures of anxiety and busyness.

It is interesting to see the same understanding of the expansive and liberating power of joy in Fr Dumitru Staniloae's exposition of the commentary on the Divine Liturgy of St Maximus the Confessor, one of the richest of Byzantine texts on this subject.

> For St Maximus action and knowledge are always linked with the enthusiasm which in worship gives birth to song. This hymn of worship expands the active and cognitive powers of the soul, widens the horizons of what is known and what can be known. . . . There are powers of action and knowledge latent in joy. And there are possibilities of joy latent in the constructive action which truly increases the reality of things, and in the developing knowledge of that reality. The good and true reality is full of joy.[7]

If such a linking of enthusiasm and praise with thought and action had been more common in our Western theology, we should be in a better position to respond constructively and with discernment to movements of enthusiasm and religious feeling when they arise.

However that may be, it is very striking to see how Hooker insists that it is the anticipation of the ultimate joy of the Kingdom which gives rise to the outward dignity and splendour of Christian worship. I believe that one could show that the use of outward symbolism in worship in any particular Christian tradition, though it is undoubtedly influenced by purely social and cultural factors, is in direct proportion to the faith of the tradition that in worship, the end is really present and made known.

For if those principal works of God, the memory whereof we are to celebrate at such times, be but certain tastes and says as it were of that final benefit, wherein our perfect felicity and bliss lieth folded up, seeing that the presence of the one doth direct our cogitations, thoughts and desires, towards the other, it giveth surely a kind of life and addeth inwardly no small delight to those so comfortable expectations, when the very outward countenance of what we presently do, representeth after a sort that also where-unto we tend. . . .[8]

Notice that it is the 'outward countenance' of what we do, which gives life and adds inward delight to our celebration of the acts of God. The outward element, far from weighing down the inward, making it formal and heavy, adds life and inner delight to what, if it remained merely mental and inward, would be incomplete. Man is a complex unity, of body as well as soul, of feeling as well as thinking. All his faculties are to be drawn into the service and praise of God.

In the light of such considerations as these we can give full weight to the well-known words in which Hooker sums up the whole of his defence of the celebration of the festivals of the Christian year. 'They are the splendour and outward dignity of our religion'; the manifestation within time and space of the glory which is in God, in which even here and now man can, in a measure, participate, the glory which shall in the end be all in all. They are 'forcible witnesses of ancient truth', powerful aids to that making of *anamnesis,* that act of remembering by which the people of God constantly rediscover their calling, and men and women recall their true nature in that memory of God, in which we remember that we are indeed remembered. They are 'provocations to the exercise of all piety', incitements to the exercise of liberality towards our fellow men which can subvert and overthrow the laws of economic determinism, and at the same time a stimulus to that going out from himself in love towards God, in which man gives voice to the praise of all creation. They are 'on earth everlasting records and memorials, wherein they which cannot be drawn to hearken unto that we teach, may only by looking upon what we do, in a manner read whatsoever we believe.'[9] They are celebrated on earth, that is to say, here in this particular time and situation; but they are also everlasting, because even within time they partake of something which is beyond time; they are happenings which speak in their totality of rest, bounty and praise, proclaiming the richness of the mercies of God; they are outward and social events which can be seen by all, not only by the articulate and verbal who read books and listen to sermons, but by 'the very simplest and rudest', the least articulate and verbal, for whom here, as in other places, Hooker is particularly concerned. It is small wonder that, with such a theology behind them, the Anglicans of the seventeenth century should have treasured their threatened festivals. Nor is it surprising that English travellers to the Middle East at this period recognised the vital importance of the observance of the Church's festivals for the maintenance of the faith of Orthodox Christians under Turkish pressure and persecution. Those who have been behind the iron curtain in our own day, will, no doubt, have had similar impressions.

We have been quoting from one small section of Hooker's consideration of the Puritan objections to the Book of Common Prayer, and we have seen how, implicit in his reply, is a whole vision of man in relation to God, man as a creature made to find his fulfilment in God, and indeed already finding that fulfilment through the whole of his life, bodily and social, as well as inward and personal; finding that fulfilment focused in his participation in the Church's worship. Here is a vision of man rejoicing in the whole of God's creation, and offering the praise of that creation, on behalf of all. Hooker is the kind of thinker who, despite the qualifications and complexities of his thought, in the end sees the unity and coherence of all things. As Loyer points out his whole theology of prayer and sacrament is based on and culminates in his understanding of the union and communion of God and man in Christ.

> The great [Christological] passages on the divine participation and presence, that is to say on the reciprocal relation of God and man, complete naturally those passages which define the relation of teaching to prayer. The internal logic which extends the mystery of the Word and Prayer into the mystery of the Eucharist becomes clear to the reader. This line of thought makes the Eucharistic sacrament the completion of the liturgical celebration, the theology of the Incarnation the crown of the theology of the Word and Prayer.[10]

Thus along with this understanding of the worship of the Church, linked with it and supporting it, there grows an understanding of man as made for God, with the desire for God planted in his very nature. 'Prayer if we grasp it in its true movement, is a recapitulation of our humanity which we offer to God. . . . Man is desire, movement towards his true end which is God; his being is prayer, it has the substance and content of prayer even if not its form. It is for each one of us to give it this form by the offering of desire.'[11] The desire for God is in the nature of man. What makes man to be man is the longing always to be going beyond himself into God. But this longing can be fulfilled only in the gift of God, which goes beyond all that we could ask or think. This gift we receive even now in faith, in hope and in love, by which, however feebly and intermittently, we already grasp the gift of himself which God makes to us. So in one of his most amazing paragraphs Hooker can speak of

> faith, the principal object whereof is that eternal Verity which hath discovered the treasures of hidden wisdom in Christ; of hope, the highest object whereof is that everlasting goodness which in Christ doth quicken the dead

and of

> charity, the final object whereof is that incomprehensible Beauty which shineth in the countenance of Christ, the Son of Living God . . . the first of which beginning here with a weak apprehension of things not seen, endeth with an intuitive vision of God in the world to come, the second beginning here with a trembling expectation of things far removed and as yet but only heard of, endeth with a real and actual fruition of that which no tongue can express; the third beginning here with a weak inclinaton of heart towards him unto whom we are not able to approach, endeth with endless union the mystery whereof is higher than the reach of the thoughts of men.[12]

Consider for a moment that it is beauty which is the final term of this ascent. Beyond and through the eternal verity, beyond and through the everlasting goodness, in some way including them, there shines the incomprehensible beauty of God. Here indeed we see something of the depth of meaning to be found in the title of the Orthodox Church's anthology of spiritual and theological writings, the *Philokalia*, the love of the divine beauty. Here we see why one of the greatet contemporary representatives of that tradition, Alexander Solzhenitsyn, in his Nobel Prize speech, in which he speaks of the 'unshakable nature of goodness and the indivisible nature of truth', can yet first of all appeal to Dostoevsky's enigmatic saying, 'Beauty will save the world.'[13] Here we see why the *Song of Songs* has always had, and will always have, a privileged place at the heart of Christian prayer and devotion. We are reminded of the reply of the Carmelite nun which so delighted St John of the Cross. When he asked her in what her prayer consisted, she replied, 'In considering the beauty of God and in rejoicing that he has such beauty.'[14]

Is it any wonder that Hooker thinks that the Church's worship should reflect in every possible way this divine glory, and that his thought should be filled with a kind of adoring wonder, which exclaims, 'Blessed be God that he is God, only and divinely like himself.'[15] Here at the heart of the Church's worship we find the absolute gratuity alike of God's gift of himself to us, and of our answering gift of ourselves to him. Here is a true continuation of that tradition of prayer and thanksgiving which has its roots in the Psalms, and which expresses itself so richly in the opening of St Paul's epistles. We find here that paradoxical union of inner and outer, of corporate and personal, of simplicity and splendour which marks the great tradition of Christian worship, and which unites into one the many and varied faculties of man's being, as they find their integration and fulfilment in participation in the divine life.

IV

It has often been said that the style and language of the Book of Common Prayer, like that of the Latin rite from which so much of it comes, is reserved and ordered, rather than ecstatic and exuberant; and that is indeed true. The structures and forms are in general

simple and avoid elaboration. There is a noble restraint and brevity
in Cranmer's translation of the Latin collects, expanded though some
of them are. The contrast with the luxuriance of the Byzantine rite,
with its wealth of poetic hymnody, is striking. Again it is evident
that balance and moderation are characteristic of the style of Hooker
as well as of the content of his thought. But neither the restraint of
the one nor the moderation of the other can disguise the awe-
inspiring mystery of God's love which lies at the heart of the Gospel,
and which is conveyed to us in the great tradition of Christian
worship. It is a mystery in which man is caught up, taken out of
himself into God, in which the whole creation is involved, in which
the heavenly powers participate. As Charles Wesley sings,

> Let earth and heaven combine
>   Angels and men agree,
> To praise in songs divine
>   The incarnate Deity,
> Our God contracted to a span
>   Incomprehensibly made man. [16]

There is perhaps no department of theology more neglected or
despised at the present day than angelology. Yet if we look at the
texts which have been used in Christian worship from the time of the
apostles until now, nothing is more evident than the belief that our
worship on earth is united with the worship of Heaven, that the
powers of Heaven are at worship with us.

> While the army above
> Overwhelm'd by his love
> The Trinity sings
> With their faces enwrapp'd in their shadowing wings,
> Holy Father, we cry,
> Holy Son, we reply
> Holy Spirit of grace
> And extol the Three-One in a rapture of praise. [17]

If there is a point where, in order to rediscover the fullness of

Christian worship, we need to recover the continuity of tradition, it is surely this one. The powers of Heaven; how are we to interpret them? With the aid of concepts drawn from Jungian depth-psychology? With the aid of the traditions of Islam and of the further East? How Hooker would have rejoiced to know those traditions! Is this perhaps one of the places where the experience of the charismatic movement could be fruitful, opening up intuitive and imaginative capacities in us which our civilisation has tended to inhibit? There are many unanswered questions to be explored.

But here again we can find a starting point in Hooker, to whom this question about the service of angels with men seems to have been of special significance. In a passage in Book I, where he cites Aristotle, 'the mirror of human wisdom', and an Orphic text, in addition to Scripture, he speaks of the angels, and remarks 'that our Saviour himself, being to set down the perfect idea of that which we are to pray and wish for on earth, did not teach to pray and wish for more than only that here it might be with us, as with them it is in heaven.'[18] And in Book V we find how seriously he takes the participation of the angels in the worship of the Church on earth: 'For what is the assembling of the Church to learn, but the receiving of angels descended from above? What to pray, but the sending of angels upwards? His heavenly inspirations and our holy desires are so many angels of intercourse and commerce between God and us.'[19] On his death-bed, Walton tells us, Hooker was meditating on the nature and the number of the angels, 'and their blessed obedience and order, without which peace could not be in heaven; and oh that it might be so on earth.'[20]

Certainly here is a sign of the gratuitous glory of the divine being and action, which we adore with angels and archangels and all the company of Heaven. Here is a sign of the opening of man's eyes and mind to larger horizons which we affirm when we proclaim that Heaven and earth alike are full of God's glory. If the tradition which the Book of Common Prayer conveys to us can allow us to enter into the meaning and the mystery of these affirmations, then indeed we may know that we are entering into that tradition of life which is given us in the Holy and Life-giving Spirit. If it conveys to us something of that joy which the world can neither give nor take away, then we may recognise that here indeed is a participation in

that life which is the life of God, which is made ours in Jesus Christ
our Lord.

NOTES

1. Olivier Loyer. *L'Anglicanisme de Richard Hooker, Essai sur sa pensée philosophique, politique et théologique.* A doctoral Thesis presented in the University of Paris in 1977
2. A phrase from the Moscow Statement of the Anglican-Orthodox Joint Doctrinal Commission's meeting in 1976. *Anglican-Orthodox Dialogue,* 1977, p. 91
3. cf. Alexander Schmemann's book, *The World as Sacrament*
4. *The Works of Richard Hooker,* edited by John Keble, 1836, Vol. I. pp. xci–xcii
5. ibid., Vol. II, p. 383 (V, lxix, 3)
6. ibid., p. 405 (V, lxxi, 10)
7. St Maximus the Confessor. *Mystagogia; Introduction and Commentary by Fr Dumitru Staniloae* (in modern Greek), 1973, pp. 240–1
8. op. cit., p. 386 (V, lxx, 4)
9. ibid., pp. 406–7 (V, lxxi, 11)
10. op. cit., p. 447
11. ibid., p. 469
12. op. cit., Vol. I, pp. 261–2 (I, xi, 6)
13. Aleksandr Solzhenitsyn. *Critical Essays and Documentary Materials,* edited by J. B. Dunlop, Richard Haugh and Alexis Klimoff, 1975, pp. 559 and 572
14. See *The Complete Works of St John of the Cross,* ed. E. Allison Peers, 1934–5
15. A phrase attributed to Hooker's younger contemporary, John Donne
16. Charles Wesley. *Methodist Hymn Book,* 142
17. Charles Wesley, quoted in *A Rapture of Praise* (ed. H. A. Hodges and A. M. Allchin), 1966, p. 47
18. op. cit., Vol. I, p. 212 (I, iv, 1)
19. ibid., Vol. II, p. 115 (V, xxiii, 1)
20. ibid., Vol. I, p. 85

8

Apostolic Order: Bearer of the Spirit

In a little, out-of-the-way cemetery in a remote corner of North
Wales, there is a gravestone commemorating three people, two
brothers and a sister who died in their twenties within a few years of
one another, in the years after the First World War. On it are the
lines:

Marwolaeth Mair a Willie a Rhisiart
Gwna i reswm dewi
Ond fydd ddichon fodloni
A gweld trefn mewn galw tri.

The death of Mary and William and Richard,
Makes reason mute;
But faith makes it possible to accept
And to see order in the calling of the three.[1]

The author was a local farmer and Methodist deacon who died in
1960 at the age of 88. In this verse we see what can be done when
there is a strict form and a living tradition. In the works of an
otherwise unknown craftsman in words, a great, a universal statement has been made. One thinks, by comparison, of the poverty and
emptiness of most of the occasional verses which appear on tomb-
stones in the English-speaking areas of Britain.

These lines bring a judgement on many of the unquestioned
assumptions of our age, assumptions which are so much a part of us

that we hardly notice their existence. I do not speak primarily of their content, though that is remarkable enough, but about their shape, their order, in the original of course much more than in translation, a masterpiece of compression and balance. Only within the conventions of a strict poetic form would it be possible to say so much, so directly in so brief a space. Indeed form and content are inseparable here. Only on the basis of a firmly held faith would it be possible to see order in such tragic waste, to give order and worth to such an apparent negation of all worth. Strict forms allied to a strong sense of tradition do not necessarily inhibit and repress the gifts of inspiration. Quite the reverse; when such structures still exist and are truly understood they may release men from their constricting individual limitations, may make possible in unlikely places acts of a surpassing excellence. To create a work of this quality, the writer, the sculptor, the musician must be prepared to die to himself, so that the splendour of the thing may be revealed.

I

Apostolic order; bearer of the Spirit, the two halves of this title might be taken to sum up and pin-point things which our world takes to be irreconcilable. On the one side, 'the dead hand of tradition', the constrictions of an ancient institution; on the other side, freedom of the Spirit, the spontaneity and vitality of life; what can they have in common? These oppositions, which our society makes so easily, are built into our way of looking at things, into our expectation of how things will be. The media-men will want to have us docketed and pigeon-holed before we can turn round; conservative or progressive, which will you choose to be? These oppositions, so unthinkingly made, are affronted by the whole life and being of the Church. By everything that it is and does, when it is true to its nature and its calling, it shows that the opposites belong together, that we cannot move into the future without being able to remember the past, that the way to freedom of action lies through a willingness to accept discipline. Thus the Church holds up to us a different, more complex and more satisfying vision of the nature of man. The apostolic order which characterises holy Church and which anchors it in the original events of the Gospels is indeed a thing which carries death within it. But it is a death which brings us to life; which leads to the coming of the Spirit who is Lord of life. For it is in the life-giving death of Jesus Christ that death is overcome, that the Spirit is made free.

What can we mean in practice by such cryptic assertions? In particular what is it that we want to say about the episcopate as the vehicle of apostolic order, the bearer of the Holy Spirit, one of the structures in the whole complex of the Church's life which enables men to pass from death into life, by enabling them to live in love together?

We must begin by making some rather obvious observations about the present situation of Anglicans on this topic. Anglicans tend at present to be very defensive and apologetic about episcopacy, and for some quite respectable reasons. Apart from the general suspicion of all old institutions, of all authority figures, of all father-hood, which characterises our times, there are special causes for a certain amount of Anglican unease at this point. We are aware that in the past we seem to have put too much emphasis on it. We are afraid that in our attempts to assert the apostolic origins and authority of this office we have said more than the evidence warrants about the way in which bishops succeeded to the apostles. Above all, we are uncomfortably aware that in the past we have tended to use this doctrine as a stick to beat others over the head with. It has not so much been the positive meaning of episcopacy which we have valued, as its convenience as a way of distinguishing ourselves from other 'non-episcopal' communions, and then of looking down on them with some disdain. When articles of Christian faith are used in this way, as too often they have been in the centuries of polemic, used that is not to construct but to destroy, then automatically they begin to go bad on us, to become hardened and distorted, to lose their true meaning and purpose.

To acknowledge these tendencies in the past, indeed to repent of them, need not make us lose sight of the truths which still lie hidden behind them. If in the past we stressed episcopacy in an unbalanced way, it was because we tended to see it in isolation rather than because we overestimated its value. There were popular handbooks on the Anglican position which seemed to make the doctrine of apostolic succession the one foundation on which all else in Christian faith and life was built. We need to see the episcopate as being one element in the whole structure of faith and life which developed in the second and third centuries, and which contains the canon of Scripture, the creeds, the sacramental and liturgical tradition of the Church, as well as the apostolic ministry. When we so see it, then we can see that in relation to those other things, as part of a greater whole, it is hard to exaggerate its importance. Similarly while we may repudiate over-simple notions of how the bishops are the successors of the apostles, while we may be glad to have arrived at a more flexible attitude towards Church order today, by recognising the probable variety of structures which marked the first generations of the Church, nevertheless we cannot help recognising that by the second century the threefold ordering of the ministry had emerged into something like the position it has held ever since. We may well conclude that this was a process which took place under the guidance of the Holy Spirit. As Raymond Brown remarks: 'I do not think that tracing the appearance of the episcopate more directly to the Holy Spirit than to the historical Jesus takes away any dignity from bishops; and I suggest upon reflection that these conclusions will be scandalous chiefly to those who have never understood the real import of our oft-repeated boast that Christianity is an historical religion.'[2]

Finally our new willingness to recognise that non-episcopal churches do in fact have ministries which exercise *episcope,* which approximate more closely to the Church's traditional order than Anglicans have sometimes been willing to allow, and which may themselves have evolved under the guidance of the Spirit, need not necessarily lead to the conclusion that they are exactly the same as the ministry which we have inherited or that they can have exactly the same significance and function. Let us rather try to articulate the positive meaning of this apostolic order, this historic episcopate, not being afraid to bring out what is specific in it. In doing so, I believe it will be possible to find a way to reaffirm our faith in the essential role of the episcopate in maintaining and expressing the Church's unity and identity, its continuity of life and awareness, through space and through time, and its no less essential role in maintaining the Church's sense of itself as apostolic, sent, i.e. living not from itself but from the one who sends it. In this way we shall bring into the unity between separated Christians which is at present coming to be, something which God has given us through the centuries. We shall, as the Lambeth Conference of 1968 said:

> offer this experience in fellowship with those who have experienced the grace of the continuity of apostolic doctrine through other forms of ministry, and with those who have experienced God's grace through papal authority in the episcopal college, in the faith that God will restore the fulness of ministry in ways which we cannot yet discern.[3]

Let us then look a little more closely at these two points and see how the episcopate helps us to affirm first that the Church lives not from itself, but from its Lord, and then how it helps us to maintain and develop that sense of being sent by God through a life which crosses and transcends the barriers of time and space.

II

I shall begin by quoting two paragraphs from a book written forty years ago, which, while it could in some ways be complemented or modified, still seems to be astonishingly actual, Michael Ramsey's *The Gospel and the Catholic Church*. I quote purposely not from the chapter on the Episcopate but from the chapter on the meaning of the Church's unity which precedes the consideration of the Gospel and Church Order and the Gospel and episcopacy in the development of the book's thesis.

> United with Christ as they are by faith and Baptism, the Christians will not interpret aright their present union with him unless they constantly look back at the events whence it has sprung, and remember that these events, wrought once for all, are the source of everything that the Christians are and have and known. They are called upon not to advertise their own 'experience' but to praise God for, and to bear witness to, the historical events

wherein the Name and the glory of God were uttered in human flesh. The faithful Christian will not draw attention to himself as an interesting specimen of life in Christ, but dying to all interest in himself and his 'experiences' he will focus attention upon the redeeming acts of Christ in history, as the centre of man's prayers and praises for all time. In other words, the Church is apostolic; it looks back to the deeds of Jesus in the flesh, and through these deeds it has been 'sent into the world'.[4]

This is the calling of every Christian. In a particular way it is the calling of all who are ordained to minister the Word and Sacraments of the Gospel, who repeat the words and deeds which daily plunge us yet again into those mysterious original facts, the death and resurrection, the coming of the Spirit from which the whole Church derives its being. Above all it is the vocation of the bishop who stands at the heart of that ministry, the sign and symbol of the presence in the Church now of the original apostolic testimony and commission. The fact that we see more of the complexity of the New Testament evidence, recognise that we do not know exactly *how* apostle was succeeded by bishop, need not take from us our conviction that this ministry by its very nature points away from itself to the mystery of God, manifest in the flesh, to the mystery of the Father's raising Jesus from the dead, to the coming of the Holy Spirit at Pentecost, and reminds us that all these things are primarily made known to us not in ideas and concepts, but in the crude stuff of human history. Already at the beginning of the second century, Ignatius of Antioch in his letters expounds this with unrivalled authority. We need not say that the historic structure of ministry which we have inherited is the only way of affirming this identity of the Christian with his Lord. We can say that it does it pre-eminently, even in and through the inadequacies of those who hold office within it, discouraging a cult of personality, pointing beyond itself to the realities which lie behind it. And we cannot help noticing that at times in Christian history, when splits have taken place, the new bodies which are formed seem specially vulnerable to powerful and autocratic individuals (in the early history of British Methodism one might think of men like Jabez Bunting or John Elias).

For as Michael Ramsey goes on to point out:

From the deeds of Jesus in the flesh there springs a society which is one in its continuous life. Many kinds of fellowship in diverse places and manners are created by the Spirit of Jesus, but they all depend upon the one life. Thus each group of Christians will learn its utter dependence upon the whole Body. It will indeed be aware of its own immediate union with Christ, but it will see this experience as a part of the one life of the one family in every age and place. By its dependence upon the Church of history it will die to self-consciousness and self-satisfaction. And as with the group, so with the individual Christian; he will know his dependence upon the other members of the Body, wherein the relation of member to member and of function to function begets humility and love. The gifts that he possesses belong to the Body, and are useful only in the Body's common life. Thus through membership he dies to self-sufficing, and knows that his life in Christ exists only as a life in which all the members share.[5]

Each Christian, each local church 'dies to self-sufficing', lives in the sharing of life and love. The great emphasis on unity which we find here is not so much a unity of outward structure, though that is not excluded, as an inward unity in the exchange of understanding and knowledge, of mutual love and concern. For if there is a death to self, it is a death into life together, in the life which the Spirit brings. It is a death into a life of communion in which many different gifts are gathered into one. All that is said here about the importance of unity, about the importance of being rooted in the once-for-all death and resurrection of Jesus, needs to be completed and fulfilled by a further development of the thought of the presence of the Spirit, the continual presence of Pentecost in the Church, so that the unrepeatable events at the origins of the Church's life may become new and living in every place and every time.

For if the bishop is by his office in a pre-eminent way the centre of the Church's unity, bearing witness to the continuity of the apostolic faith and teaching, gathering his own diocese around himself, ensuring its unity with the whole Church through his own brotherly unity with his fellow-bishops, so also is he the guardian and promoter of the Church's diversity, of the great variety of gifts and insights which come to birth in the coming of the Spirit. Where there is life and growth, there is bound to be tension and change. To be rooted in the past does not mean to be held captive in the past; quite the reverse, as we see in the case of a man like Pope John XXIII. Elected to the Papacy at the age of seventy-seven he was constantly recalling the teaching he had received as a child in his peasant family and in the village church at Sotto Il Monte. And it was precisely this rootedness in the past which enabled him to be so hopeful and confident in his turning towards the present and the future, confident that God was at work now, no less than in the past.

Of course it may often be necessary to go behind what is commonly thought to be 'tradition', to jettison a lot of what is mere convention, in order to arrive at the life-giving elements in the tradition which we have received. The true Christian appeal to the past can have unexpectedly revolutionary consequences. And this is so because the past events in which the Church's life is rooted are not simply past, not simply historical. They are revelations in history of eternally present realities, Jesus Christ, the same yesterday and today and forever; the Holy Spirit, Lord and life-giver now as at the first moment of creation. These original events have an endless vitality, and draw out constantly new responses. Indeed they constantly lead us on towards the future, because the fullness of their power and meaning will be revealed only in the consummation of all things. The Church needs above all in our times to learn how to turn towards the future with hope. The times in which we live demand a newness of response, a willingness to experiment, a need to see new things and to see old things in new ways. We need to be open to the impulses of the Holy Spirit, and it is certain that different ones of us will see different things as needing to be done. It is surely one of the most striking features of St Paul's teaching about the Holy Spirit, that the Spirit is presented as at one and the same time the source of the Church's unity, and of the Church's diversity. There are many different gifts and functions. The bishop as the servant and bearer of the Spirit must seek to do justice to these two aspects of the Spirit's work, to maintain together in one body, individuals and movements with very different visions of what is most urgently necessary.

III

One of the finest statements of this function of the bishop as guardian of the Church's inclusiveness is to be found in the sermon which Richard Church preached at an episcopal consecration in 1869, (the consecration of George Moberly to be Bishop of Salisbury). Precisely because it comes out of a situation different from, though not less difficult than, our own, it can speak to us across the years. The preacher speaks of the role of the Episcopate in sustaining the Church's continuity through the centuries.

> Other organisations have with more or less success kept up Christianity; but they date from particular times and belong to particular places, and are the growth of special circumstances. Only this has been everywhere where Christianity has been; only this belongs peculiarly to Christianity, as a whole. A bishop is a representative person, and he represents much more than the authority and claims of anything present or local; his functions and commission are of the most ancient derivation, and of the widest recognition; he is an organ of a great movement, the officer of a great kingdom which has been going on since the beginning of Christianity, and allows itself no bounds but the world ... he recalls, even now, the almost obliterated image of a once embodied and visible communion of Christians, still able to be one.[6]

But it is not only this historical character of the episcopate which is of importance. He goes on:

> The episcopate represents the Christianity of history; it represents further, the Christianity of the general Church, as distinguished from the special opinions and views of doctrine which assert their claims in it. Its long lines tie together the Christian body in time; they are scarcely less a bond connecting the infinite moral and religious differences which must always be in the body of the Church.

The bishop stands for the ordinary everyday things of Christian life and teaching. 'Those mean despised truths that everyone thinks he is sufficiently seen in.' He stands for something larger than particular interests and enthusiasms. Within the Church

> there is sure to be much divergence; how can there fail to be, when the soul has free play, and opens into real life, on the tremendous and absorbing objects of religion? Who too can doubt the vast part which belongs to this independent action of individuals?—the incalculable service rendered by individual desire of excellence and hatred of evil, by the devotion, the charity, the spirit of reform, the love of truth, in private men.

Where would the Church be without the great movements of renewal within it? The preacher cites monasticism, the mendicant orders, Puritanism, 'the many phases of nonconformity', the Society of Jesus, as examples of such movements within the history of the Church; vital but in themselves not enough. 'There is one thing these great movements cannot do; they cannot fill the great compass of man's nature and aims and needs. They are one-sided; they must leave much untouched; and further they would, if they were strong enough, destroy all that they cannot assimilate or subdue.'[7]

In all this the bishop has a central, moderating role to play, holding together things that will otherwise too easily fall apart, reminding the ardent, the enthusiasts, of the existence of the life of humdrum Christian congregations unmarked by any special characteristic. He must speak on their behalf.

> Others might have newer, perhaps deeper, perhaps more eventful things to say. He was there to remind Christians of that vast, wide, spiritual society which was meant to embrace us all; of the force and value of what is common, and public, and continuous, and customary. He was there to bind together in each age the old and the new, the weak and the strong; to witness, amid the vicissitudes of individual thought and energy, for something which, with less show, wears better and lasts longer; for a common inheritance of faith and religion, which needs to be filled up in its outlines by private conviction and activity, but without

which everything private risks becoming one-sided in ideas, and cramped in sympathy, and at last poor in heart.[8]

Certainly Dean Church's vision of the bishop's role is not un-influenced by the position of the bishop in the nineteenth-century Church of England. A bishop living in a minority Church in the late twentieth century will necessarily experience things in somewhat different ways. But when all allowance has been made for differing social and cultural situations, there remains much in this picture of the bishop's office which is genuinely catholic and apostolic, and not particularly Anglican or even Victorian. We are reminded irre-sistibly of two sayings attributed to Pope John: 'The Church is not an archaelogical museum, but the ancient fountain which slakes the thirst of the generation of today as she did of the generations of the past.' And again: 'The bishop is always a public fountain.' Behind this striking picture of a fountain of water in a dry and thirsty land, we can surely see one of the greatest of all the biblical images for God and for man, made and renewed in God's image and likeness. The man of faith is to be a man of rock-like quality, Peter, firm, steadfast, immovable. Yet this faithfulness is far from being inert or unfruitful. For out of the rock there flows a spring of living water, of water welling up into eternal life. From the eternal stability of the Word there comes the ceaseless creativity of the Spirit. Thus the bishop is to be the man for all seasons, the one around whom things can find their order. Perhaps he is not himself the prophet or the innovator. 'Others may have newer, perhaps deeper, perhaps more eventful things to say.' Rather he is the co-ordinator, the reconciler, the leader who can hold together in a fruitful juxtaposition people and tendencies which will otherwise too easily run into separation from one another.

This role is neither passive nor neutral. True, the bishop will sometimes have to be patient rather than active, to allow things to happen and to take their own time, rather than seeking to impose himself immediately upon the situation. With his encouragement, experiments can take place, the new be recognised in ways which do not break but enliven the life of the whole body. By his presence and approval he will be able to encourage initiatives in others, to make possible new lines of action, using his authority to build and not to break down. But he himself will have very definitely to cultivate an ecumenical, a universal habit of mind, looking beyond his own diocese, beyond his own region, to what is happening in the Church across the world, seeking to be sensitive to the movements of the Spirit. As Lambeth 1968 remarked:

> The principle underlying *collegiality* is that the apostolic calling, responsibility and authority are an inheritance given to the whole body or college of bishops. Every individual bishop has therefore a responsibility both as a member of this college and as chief pastor in his diocese. In the latter capacity he exercises direct oversight over the people committed to his charge. In the former he shares with his brother bishops throughout the world a concern for the well-being of the whole church. [9]

To say this is not so difficult. To do it is something different. It is easy to let ourselves be pulled to pieces by the tensions and conflicts in the Church, by the tensions and conflicts between the Church and the world. We cannot forget that as recently as 1977 the archbishop of one of the Churches of the Anglican communion gave his life on behalf of his people. To stand in a central, representative position will at times be a crucifying occupation. We were never promised anything else. 'A servant is not above his master.' Indeed only so shall we be able to exercise the authority of self-giving love, the authority of the one who made himself the servant of all, and who laid down his life for his sheep. It is through Jesus's laying down of life that in the gift of the Father, the Spirit is set free. What is true for him, is in its measure true for his ministers. 'Give thy blood and receive the Spirit,' as the ancient monastic saying has it. Here is the only way forward towards the discovery of a genuine and liberating fatherhood, towards an authority which builds up and does not destroy, towards an apostolic order which is also bearer of the Spirit.

IV

Already more than ten years ago, Olivier Clément was writing, 'The problem of fatherhood is without doubt the greatest problem of our age.' Everywhere we are witnessing the breakdown of traditional structures of authority and paternity.

> Between bad fatherhood, which is arbitrary tyranny, and bad brotherhood, which is chaos, boredom and the absence of all creative discipline, the duty of Christians is to search painfully for a living creation of a new reality in the light of the revelation of the Trinity. For the Christian cannot participate in the mystery of the divine fatherhood and witness to it validly except by living in the Son and the Holy Spirit. . . . The contemporary revolt against the father is not basically a denial of fatherhood as such but a search for a trinitarian fatherhood, lived in brotherly respect for the other, in order that the life-giving Spirit may be communicated.[10]

The search for a rediscovery of a life-giving fatherhood is, still, one of the most urgent tasks of our contemporary civilisation. To be a father in God, as every priest and still more every bishop is called to be, is in this sense something central to the life and struggle of our society, though it is not in general recognised to be so. To be in any Christian sense father in God, must mean a readiness to give oneself wholly, to go out from oneself in love, to die in order that the other may live. This is what the Father has done in coming out from himself in the Son and in the Spirit. If we can go out from ourselves in this way, in the strength of the love which comes from God alone, then we find that through death life is made free, the Spirit is imparted and received. We are united with Christ alike in life and death, in life through death. 'Always bearing about in the body the dying of the Lord Jesus, that the life also of Jesus might be made manifest in our body.'[11]

A fatherhood, an authority lived in brotherly respect for the others, with a real perception of where they are and what is happening within them, will be a costly, demanding thing. It will involve the action of one who is a priest, who goes to be with the other one, who identifies himself with him, rather than the action of a moralist who judges from afar. Only through this identification can the Spirit be made free. This is not the abandonment of the role of father, a temptation which is always with us, and which, however attractive it may seem, in the end involves a betrayal of those who look for newness of life, a betrayal which leads to chaos, boredom, the absence of all creative discipleship. Nor is it a return to the old authoritarian role, which relied on force of personality or on force of social pressure to arrive at an outward conformity, a merely external handing on of the tradition. It is something more costly than that, purchased with nothing less than the offering of life, which involves the constant risk of human freedom. Only in freedom can the Spirit's power be truly made known. It is the revelation of a fatherhood in which man's part is to be transparent to the action of the one Father of all. And it can bring us even here and now from death into that life of which St John speaks when he says that we know that we have passed from death to life, because we love the brethren.

It is in that love which comes from God but which is rooted in the hearts and minds and wills of men and women, that the apostolic office can become truly Spirit-bearing. Only through death can we come to life. For most of us the struggle with evil, with the powers of denial and destruction in the world, will be outwardly undramatic; it will not take on the open character which it had in the case of Archbishop Janani Luwum. Very often it will be a hidden conflict, waged within our own hearts as we 'uncover beneath the social and moral expressions of evil, their satanic roots, and our own fundamental complicity with them.' But deeper than the darkness which we find within ourselves is the light of the Incarnate Word, which shines in the darkness and is not overcome by it. Stronger than the separations which we make is the love of the Crucified Lord who descended into the depths, into all the hells, inner and outer, that men can make for themselves and for their fellows, in order to plant there the seeds of faith and hope and love. It is as we are learning through the creative gift of divine forgiveness to hope against hope even within ourselves, even on account of ourselves, that we shall be enabled to become men of forgiveness, men of the creative power of love, those who have been given not the spirit of fear, but of power, and love, and soberness. As Olivier Clément writes, 'The Church is the place, in a world dominated by death, where life is always opening itself, where our freedom is set free in the Spirit, and receives its content in creative love.' The bishop is the one who stands at the heart of the Church, himself seeking constantly to be open to God in the very centre of his being, so that through that centre the life-giving power of the Spirit may be present in his whole life, and through him present in the midst of God's people.

NOTES

1. I am indebted to my friend Professor Bedwyr Lewis Jones for the text and translation of this verse
2. R. E. Brown. *Priest and Bishop, Biblical Reflections,* 1970, p. 73
3. *The Lambeth Conference 1968: Resolutions and Reports,* p. 127
4. A. M. Ramsey. *The Gospel and the Catholic Church* 2nd ed., 1955, pp. 43–4
5. ibid., p. 44
6. R. W. Church. *Pascal and Other Sermons,* 1886, pp. 105–6
7. ibid., pp. 108–9
8. ibid., pp. 11–2
9. op. cit., p. 137
10. From the article 'Purification by Atheism', by Olivier Clément, in *Orthodoxy and the Death of God,* ed. A. M. Allchin, 1971, pp. 33–4
11. II Corinthians 4: 10

Comprehensiveness and the Mission of the Church

The concept of comprehensiveness is one whose meaning and value seem self-evident to the majority of Anglicans. The word is used to describe the legitimate diversity within the Church. When it is used in conjunction with the word mission, it clearly speaks of the inclusive character of the family of God into' whose unity all mankind is to be called. Indeed, in this context comprehensiveness becomes almost synonymous with Catholicity, and speaks of the universality of the Church's mission to people of all times and all places.

It is when Anglicans come to meet Christians of other traditions than their own, by no means only Orthodox, that they are forced to examine their position more closely. For they find that the idea of comprehensiveness is by no means as easily accepted as they might expect. The word itself seems to be of comparatively recent usage in theological contexts, though the idea of 'comprehension' already appears in the latter part of the seventeenth century in relation to the attempts to keep together Anglicans and Protestant Nonconformists within a single national Church. Again the word is not easy to translate into other European languages, and the idea of *doctrinal* comprehensiveness is one which has been strange to most other Christian traditions. Thus, we are forced to ask, is this doctrinal comprehensiveness, which is now so widely regarded as the characteristic feature of post-Reformation Anglicanism, only a product of the last century, or is it typical of the whole of Anglican history from the sixteenth century onwards? It is evident that there are very large historical and theological problems here, which we can only begin to consider in this chapter.

I

Before beginning our brief historical enquiry into Anglican comprehensiveness, we ought to recognise that the fact that it is natural for an Anglican to begin in this way is in itself of great significance for our relations with the Orthodox. On the one side it suggests a certain similarity between our two traditions, in so far as in both, what the Church does, in worship and in common life, and what the Church has done in the past are vital for the discovery of the meaning of its faith and teaching. But on the other side, it also suggests one of the major reasons for difference between our two traditions. It is not only that Western and Eastern Christendom have very different historical experiences, but that more profoundly they have a different relationship to the historical development of the worlds in which they are set. One of the major reasons for the apparent untidiness of the Anglican Churches in doctrinal matters is their very close involvement with the currents of historical development in the English-speaking world. Anglicans are involved in history and *open* to history in a way which seems scandalous to many Orthodox. The Orthodox seem withdrawn from history, standing apart from its vicissitudes in a way which seems scandalous to many Anglicans. When everyone in the West speaks about *aggiornamento*, the Orthodox have the impression that we are all modernists. When in the Orthodox East everyone speaks of tradition the Western Christian has the impression that Orthodoxy is caught in a kind of immobilism.

This difference of emphasis between East and West—for it is one of the points where all Western Churches would be united—has been remarked upon by theologians of many different Churches. If, as some Orthodox theologians admit, the Orthodox line has within it the danger of sclerosis, at the same time it also has great strength. There is a certain immediacy of contact with the Gospel, with the sources of Christian faith and life, which continues under the Orthodox Church's elaborate exterior, and which constitutes one of its most powerful attractions for many non-Orthodox Christians. In some ways the Orthodox East seems at its heart to have a more direct and intuitive grasp of the central realities of the Christian tradition than either of the two main families of Western Christendom. On the other hand in the practical working out of the implications of that faith, and in the intellectual analysis of its meaning, it seems as if the West has attempted and achieved more. Some of the greatest theologians of Anglicanism, a Joseph Butler, a William Temple, or in our own day an Ian Ramsey, have given themselves to the exposition of the faith in the terms presented by their own times. Hence comes part at least of our doctrinal comprehensiveness, of the untidy and open nature of our theological tradition. But Anglicanism, like the rest of the Christian West, has had, and increasingly will have, its problem not only of being related to the contemporary world, but also of being related to its Gospel origins. If Orthodoxy has the danger of sclerosis and rigidity, the West, particularly perhaps at the present moment, has the danger of dispersion and assimilation by the world. It may be that the term 'comprehensiveness', at least as we commonly understand it, will provide only part of the answer to this problem of interpretation and tradition, of how the one faith is translated into all tongues, and of how the Church while being wholly in the world and for the world yet remains the sacrament of the presence of a kingdom which is not of this world.

We have been thinking here of comprehensiveness, i.e. of diversity of theological system and teaching, as it results from the Church's openness to the developments of the world around it, and the demands which follow for re-interpretation and re-statement. But the doctrinal comprehensiveness of the Anglican Communion has in the past been more obviously linked with the Church of England's comparative openness to both sides in the great sixteenth-century division within Western Christendom. It has moved more obviously on the Catholic-Protestant axis, than on the Liberal-Conservative one, and been conditioned more by the divisions within the Christian family than by its relationship with the outside world. But both elements have always been present, and though Orthodox theologians will certainly want to ask how it is that two mutually conflicting doctrines of the sacraments and the ministry can exist within one Church, it may well be that they will be even more anxious to know how those who hold to old formulations, and those who feel impelled to abandon them, can really be confessing a common faith. We shall certainly have to consider both aspects of the problem.

II

We must turn now to a brief consideration of the history of this question. The comprehensiveness of the Church of England, and then of the Anglican Communion, can be understood only within the context of the development of Western Christendom as a whole since the sixteenth century. In a situation in which the old unity of the Western Church had disintegrated, it was evidently to the advantage of rulers to comprehend as many of their subjects as possible within the boundaries of a national Church. If possible it was desirable to include in such a unity both the reforming Catholics and the more moderate Protestants; such at least seems to have been the aim of Elizabeth I in England, as it was of John III in Sweden.

It would be wrong to see the policy of Elizabeth as the sole factor lying behind the nascent comprehensiveness of the Church of England, but it would also be impossible to ignore it. While her hopes of including all in one institution proved unrealisable, it would probably be true to say that the Anglican settlement, as it existed in the first half of the seventeenth century, was slightly but significantly more comprehensive doctrinally than were the corresponding Protestant settlements in say Holland or Scandinavia. Already in the Anglicanism of this period one can see the beginnings of what were later to become the three main tendencies, schools or parties which have characterised its subsequent development. There is a strongly Reformation element, a tentatively Catholic element, having still some links with the Reformed Catholicism of Henry VIII, and an Erasmian humanist element, which begins again to make itself known, though the extent to which these differences subsequently developed would have greatly surprised the

theologians of this period. However in the largeness of view of a
Richard Hooker or a Lancelot Andrewes, which refused to follow out
the increasing strictness of Calvinist developments and which turns
to the Fathers and the consensus of the first five centuries in an
attempt to disentangle essential from inessential matters of faith,
one can already see something recognisably typical of later Anglican
developments.

This eirenic policy of distinguishing between fundamental and
secondary matters, whether of faith or practice, and insisting only on
the former, reflected the moderation of the Anglican formularies
themselves. The Prayer Book and Articles, though not intentionally
ambiguous, were moderate in their demands. They did not define
more matters than contemporary controversy demanded. And even
such definitions as they made were, for the most part, imposed only
upon the clergy, as the teachers of the Church. The laity were not
required to assent to more than the Creeds and the catechism.

The Civil War came as a blow to this limited comprehensiveness.
The violence of the controversies of the Commonwealth period led to
a reaction in 1662, which had the effect of limiting the inclusiveness
of the Church of England considerably. Neither in 1662 nor in 1689
were the proposals for 'comprehension' accepted. It may well be that
the exclusion first of the Puritans and then of the Non-Jurors was
one of the major factors which led to the weakness of the Church in
England in the eighteenth century. It certainly seems to be linked
with the Church's failure to 'comprehend', John Wesley, in whose
formation both Puritan and Non-Juring influences had been strong.

If, towards the end of the eighteenth century, comprehensiveness
again begins to characterise the Church of England, the credit must
largely go to those Evangelicals who stayed within its borders, and
insisted that their then unfashionable Calvinist interpretations of the
Prayer Book and Articles were correct. It was not until the middle of
the nineteenth century that their position was finally secured, and by
that time the development of the Oxford Movement and the beginnings of liberal, critical theology, were making openings towards a
comprehensiveness greater than any known in earlier Anglican history.

The century from 1850 to 1950 may be said to have marked a
high-water mark of Anglican comprehensiveness in the form in

which it is familiar to us. At times the different schools of thought have organised themselves into something like political parties, and the opposition between Catholic, Evangelical and Liberal movements has often been intense. The bounds of comprehension were enlarged, and at times it seemed as if the Church could hardly stand the strain.

It may well be important for us to point out that the differences within Anglicanism, even when they were at their most acute, never became so absolute as they sometimes appeared to outside observers. There is, and has always been, a large body of clergy and lay people in the centre, willing to learn from the various movements in the Church, but unwilling to be wholly identified with any one of them. Moreover, for the great majority of Christian people these differences have been experienced more in matters of worship and devotion, and in questions of Christian life, than in strictly doctrinal issues. On the one side there has been and is the Evangelical love of the Bible, which leads to a whole personal religion built up around the use of the Bible, its study in private or in small groups, its meditative reading as the basis of prayer. Together with this, there is the Evangelical insistence on the necessity of personal experience and personal decision, the free commitment of faith to Jesus as Lord. If we are truly Christian there must be some conscious knowledge of the grace of God. With this goes a belief in the importance of lay initiatives within the Church, and a readiness to find God speaking in unexpected places. On the other side there is a piety centred on the liturgical worship of the Church and the frequent participation in the sacraments. Here there is a much greater stress on the authority of tradition and on the reality of the corporate life of the whole Church. We find ourselves as Christians as one of great company, we are caught up into the Communion of Saints. Here there is a correspondingly higher regard for the position of the ordained ministry within the Church and a stronger sense of the corporate character and the historical continuity of the Church's life. How far these ways are contradictory to one another, how far complementary, is a question to be explored. The majority of Anglicans now would probably be of the conviction that they can and should complement and enrich one another.

For there are a good many signs that the former situation of

Catholic and Evangelical opposition and rivalry is altering radically, and that it is often difficult to know where or how to place people in relation to the old controversies. This development within Anglicanism is, of course, closely linked with changes of a much larger kind in Christendom as a whole.

The old concept of Anglicanism as the Bridge-Church between Catholicism and Protestantism has to be modified at a time when the broken dialogue between Rome and the Reformation is being taken up everywhere along the line. It is notorious that ideas and practices often thought in the past to be exclusively Catholic are re-establishing themselves in much of Protestantism (re-discovery of liturgy, re-discovery of the monastic life, e.g.). It is even more evident that the corresponding process is taking place within Roman Catholicism, with extreme rapidity (emphasis on justification by faith, on the role of the laity, etc.). To many it seems as if the outstanding issues of the Reformation period are on the verge of being resolved. It may well be that Anglicanism, with its longer experience of an internal Catholic-Protestant dialectic, has something particular to contribute in this new situation. It certainly has no longer any kind of monopoly of the dialogue. Doctrinal comprehensiveness of the Catholic-Protestant kind is becoming characteristic of other Western Churches beside the Anglican

But while the tension between Catholic and Evangelical is manifestly diminishing in the Anglican Communion, there are some signs that the tension between those who look to the past and those who look to the future, whatever their background, is increasing, and will increase. As the rate of change in human society at large accelerates, so the problem of adaptation becomes urgent and ever more difficult for all Churches. There are at least three large areas of theological concern which touch all Churches and which are tending to strain the comprehensiveness of all of them. They are areas vitally related with Christian mission:

(*a*) the relation of the divine revelation to the images and thought forms in which it is expressed in Scripture and in the classical Christian Creeds;

(*b*) the nature of the inspiration and authority of Scripture, and the question of the authority and irreformability of the Creeds;

(*c*) the possibility of the transposition of the Church's faith, worship and life into other cultural forms, both in relation to the other great religious traditions of mankind, and also in relation to the developing technological scientific civilisation of our own century.

Here again the Anglican experience of comprehensiveness may be valuable in helping ourselves and others to see how things apparently contradictory are often complementary. But here again neither the situation nor the predicament is exclusively Anglican.

III

When we come to examine the words 'comprehend', 'comprehensive', 'comprehensiveness' more closely, we find in them a shade of meaning which too often we allow to remain undeveloped. To take some of the phrases from the definitions of the *New English Dictionary* for 'comprehensive', we find 'comprising or including much; of large content or scope', or again 'embracing many things, broad in mental grasp. sympathies or the like', or again 'containing much in small measure'. This last suggestion, of much in little, brings us back to the root meaning of comprehend, which, after the sense of grasp or understand, seems to be to sum up, or bring together into one. Here is an element of comprehensiveness which we have not greatly stressed in the past, but which may be useful both in trying to understand it for ourselves and also in explaining its meaning to theologians of other Churches. The word 'comprehensiveness' implies unity as well as diversity; it suggests inclusiveness and largeness of sympathy as well as mere variety of view; it suggests a movement of gathering and bringing into one.

This unity can be founded in nothing less than the unity of God. There is one Father, one incarnate Lord, one Holy Spirit who gathers together the one People of God. At the very heart of the Gospel there is the assurance that this mystery of unity is a living, working, reconciling thing, making men to be at one with God, at one with their fellow men, at one within themselves. If there were no true unity of faith, there could be no true unity of the Church, but only sets of divergent opinions, whose holders might, for a variety of reasons, agree to work together for practical ends. What is more, there could be no saving, life-giving knowledge of God, if all that we had was our own view of what God had done in Christ, and no God-given knowledge and love of him. Without the faith of the whole Church, the whole Christian community, the faith of the believer could be no more than an individual opinion, an individual conviction. But the Holy Spirit who opens our eyes to see Jesus as Lord and enables us in him to stand before the Father, is also he who unites us with one another in the unity of the faith and knowledge of the Son of God, liberating us from the narrowness of our own conceptions into the largeness of the Kingdom of Heaven.

It is of the utmost importance in our relations with other Churches, and in particular with the Orthodox, that we should clearly make this affirmation of the necessity for unity in faith, which is strongly implied by our constant and universal liturgical practice, and in particular by our use of the creeds in worship, but which sometimes remains as an unspoken assumption in Anglican theological writing. If we fail to do this, our doctrinal comprehensiveness could too easily appear as a mere tolerance of divergent positions, a pragmatic indifference to questions of truth. Every Anglican who has taken part in ecumenical discussions will be aware that this is how our tradition looks at times to even friendly observers from other traditions. And we should surely be less than honest with ourselves if we did not acknowledge that there is a real danger in our tradition at this point, the danger that our comprehensiveness should become static and complacent.

It seems that considerations of this kind were in the mind of the Committee of the Lambeth Conference of 1968 on Anglican-Orthodox relations. In the paragraph devoted to comprehensiveness, it says,

Comprehensiveness demands agreement on fundamentals, while tolerating disagreement on matters in which Christians may differ without feeling the necessity of breaking communion. In the mind of an Anglican, comprehensiveness is not compromise. Nor is it to bargain one truth for another. . . . Rather it implies that the apprehension of truth is a growing thing: we only gradually succeed in 'knowing the truth'. It has been the tradition of Anglicanism to contain within one body both Protestant and

Catholic elements. But there is a continuing search for the whole truth in which these elements will find complete reconciliation. Comprehensiveness implies a willingness to allow liberty of interpretation, with a certain slowness in arresting or restraining exploratory thinking. We tend to applaud the wisdom of the rabbi Gamaliel's dictum that if a thing is not of God it will not last very long (Acts 5: 38–9). Moreover we are alarmed by the sad experience of too hasty condemnation in the past (as in the case of Galileo). For we believe that in leading us into all the truth the Holy Spirit may have some surprises in store for us in the future, as he had in the past.[1]

It could be wished that signs of this continuing search were more evident in our Communion, and that when controversy breaks out on some well-worn theme, the arguments produced on both sides were less stale and stereotyped. It might be easier to commend 'comprehensiveness' to other Christians if there were more evidence of this search for reconciliation.

But if there are factors in our actual practice of comprehensiveness which are somewhat discouraging, it is on the other hand an extremely encouraging fact that the last century of Anglican history, which has been the period of greatest comprehensiveness, has also been the time of the greatest Anglican activity in the spheres both of unity and mission. We have in the life of our Church the basis for an understanding of comprehensiveness as a dynamic, reconciling reality, and of the positive value of tensions contained within one body, and it is this which we must now examine.

The comprehensiveness of the Church and of the Church's faith reflects at one and the same time the richness and fullness of the mystery of God's acts of redemption in Christ, and also the richness and diversity of the world which God has made. The wisdom of God is many-faceted, so that there are many different aspects of the divine truth to be seen, and men may approach the mystery with many different gifts and experiences. The unity of the Church is a unity of life and faith and worship in which all these different gifts and experiences are able to cohere but which no one man or system can comprehend.

In Anglicanism, the unity of life is fundamental and precedes all other unities. Anglicans are those who are willing to live together in one Church on the basis of a unity of faith, which they believe is not specifically Anglican, but simply the faith of the whole Church. This faith is defined in terms of the Bible as interpreted by tradition, and in particular by the first four Councils and the 'Catholic Creeds set in their context of Baptismal profession, patristic reasoning and conciliar decision'. The basic Christological and Trinitarian definitions of the early Church still have authority for us, even though there are many who are rightly seeking their re-interpretation. Why do we regard these dogmas as essential and these councils as authoritative? First, because they provide the way of approach to Scripture, the hermeneutical key, if you will, which enables us to discern the proportion of faith as the Bible bears witness to it; and they represent the first, crucial and, in some sense, typical transposition of the Biblical *kerygma* from one cultural world to another. Secondly, the dogmas defined at that time touch the very heart of the Christian mystery, the activity of God in Christ; they are saving truths. Their whole intention is soteriological. Thirdly, the first four Councils represent the consensus of the whole of early Christendom, and have been consistently received by the Churches ever since.

This last statement must at once be qualified, particularly with reference to the Churches which never accepted the definitions of Chalcedon. It is surely highly relevant to our own discussions with the Byzantine Orthodox, that in recent years (Aarhus 1964, Bristol 1967, Geneva 1970) there should have taken place discussions between their theologians and those of the non-Chalcedonian Churches, and that at the meeting in 1967 they should have reached such a remarkable degree of agreement. 'Ever since the fifth century,' they declared, 'we have used different formulae to confess our common faith in the One Lord Jesus Christ, perfect God and perfect Man.'[2] Here is a remarkable example of doctrinal comprehensiveness, and a readiness to acknowledge that there may be identity of faith behind apparent differences of formulation.

This unity of faith is expressed and maintained in Anglicanism, through a common tradition of worship and confession. It is the liturgical worship of the Church which has carried the faith of the Church, and it is in part for this reason that the laity feel so intensely about changes that are made in it. The place which in European Protestantism is occupied by the theological professor, and in Roman Catholicism by the Papacy, is in Anglicanism given to the Church's tradition of worship. Here again we have diversity and unity. At the present moment it is not so easy to define what unifies the different Anglican rites as in the period before liturgical revision and reform, since the Prayer Books of the various Provinces are developing, to some extent, independently of one another. However, the Lambeth Conference of 1958 suggested certain principles of liturgical revision which would characterise all Anglican attempts at reform in this field. The liturgy must be biblical, both in its doctrine, and in its constant use of the Scriptures. It must make proper provision for the ministry both of Word and of Sacraments. It must be thoroughly congregational. The whole movement of liturgical revision in Anglicanism has been based not only on the need for adaptations to new circumstances, but also on a concern for the restoration of the true proportions of the Church's tradition of worship.[3]

This common tradition of faith and worship and life is, of course, structured around a common church order. Anglicans have made this point with such insistence during the past century that it is hardly necessary to underline it here. But again we see how a given structure allows for diversity of expression, and variety of interpretation. The Lambeth Conference of 1948 sought to describe our position on this question thus:

Authority, as inherited by the Anglican Communion from the undivided Church of the early centuries of the Christian era, is single in that it is derived from a single Divine source, and reflects within itself the richness and historicity of the divine Revelation. . . . It is distributed among Scripture, Tradition, Creeds, the Ministry of the Word and Sacraments, the witness of the saints, and the *consensus fidelium,* which is the continuing experience of the Holy Spirit through his faithful people in the Church. It is thus a dispersed rather than a centralised authority, having many elements which combine, interact with, and check each other; these elements together contributing by a process of mutual support, mutual checking, and redressing of errors or exaggerations to the many-sided fullness of the authority which Christ has committed to his Church. . . . This essentially Anglican authority is reflected in our adherence to episcopacy as the source and centre of our Order, and the Book of Common Prayer as the standard of worship. Liturgy, in the sense of the offering and ordering of the public worship of God, is the crucible in which these elements of authority are fused and unified in the fellowship and power of the Holy Spirit. It is the living and ascended Christ, present in the worshipping congregation, who is the meaning and unity of the whole Church. He presents it to the Father, and sends it out on its mission.[4]

Here we have a concept of the unity in diversity of the Church's life which it would be highly interesting to discuss with our Orthodox colleagues. With its stress on the role of the Holy Spirit, with its insistence on the centrality of worship, with its refusal to locate authority precisely in one place, it has much in common with the Orthodox way of handling this question. Is there, beneath the so-evident superficial differences of Anglicanism and Orthodoxy, the untidiness of the one, the strictness of the other, the liberalism of the one, the conservatism of the other, an underlying affinity in a belief in an authority which serves freedom, and a truth which liberates? Are both sides seeking to bear witness to the life in Christ, to a gift of the Holy Spirit, which is greater than any attempt to capture it in words? 'The only authority in the Catholic Church which can ultimately preserve the truth is the power of the Holy Ghost to guide the theologians in the end to a true understanding of the faith.'[5]

It is interesting to compare the statement of 1948 with what was said on this theme in the Conference of 1968, in relation to the Thirty-Nine Articles.

The inheritance of faith which characterises the Anglican Communion is an authority of a multiple kind and . . . to the different elements which occur in the different strands of this inheritance, different Anglicans attribute different levels of authority. From this foundation arises Anglican tolerance, comprehensiveness and ordered liberty, though admittedly it makes Anglican theology variegated rather than monolithic, and informal rather than systematically deductive.[6]

After speaking of the place of the early Creeds and the Reformation formulae within this inheritance the Report goes on to speak of

> the authority given within the Anglican tradition to reason, not least as exercised in historical and philosophical inquiry, . . . To such a threefold inheritance of faith belongs a concept of authority which refuses to insulate itself against the testing of history and the free action of reason. It seeks to be a credible authority and therefore is concerned to secure historical support and to have its credentials in a shape which corresponds to the requirements of reason.[7]

In this insistence on the rights of reason in relation to faith, especially as exercised in philosophical and historical enquiry, and on the fact that the authority of the faith cannot insulate itself against the testing of history and the free action of reason, we have a striking illustration of the Anglican openness to the development of human thought and civilisation which we spoke of at the beginning of this chapter. Here is a place at which many apparent differences between ourselves and the Orthodox may arise. How, we may be asked, can we permit the critical intellect to pry into the heart of the mysteries of the faith? How, we may respond, can the Eastern Orthodox Church appear so unaffected by historical and critical inquiry?

Here again, having registered the differences, we shall have to probe deeper and ask whether underneath there is a real but less apparent similarity. It has been customary among Anglicans to attribute our more optimistic view of the role of human reason to the influence of the Greek fathers. Is there foundation for this? Have the more speculative and critical activities of Anglican thinkers been in true succession to the work of the Christian authors of the centuries before the schism of East and West? How far will the Orthodox Church own the free religious thinking of a Solovyov or a Fyodorov, certainly no less daring than the most prophetic writings of the West?

These are not questions which we can answer in advance. But I believe that as Anglicans we shall approach them with a conviction of the positive value of diversity in the Church, even in questions of doctrine, and an experience that diversity need not in itself be divisive. This does not mean that the experience of tension and disagreement within the Church is not, at times, extremely painful. There are occasions when we do not see our way forward through questions of controversy, when individuals may be deeply troubled by conflicting tendencies, and when for a time, we go forward together on an agreement to disagree, rather than on any profound vision of unity. But this experience, difficult though it is, is consistent with a corresponding conviction that 'truth is great and will prevail.' As John Macquarrie has put it,

> We believe that the best answer to deviant beliefs and practices is not to try to suppress them but to bring them into the open and, by free criticism, to show what is mistaken in them as well as learning something of the truth that is hidden in every error. No doubt there is a risk in this permissiveness, but we believe that it is a risk worth taking if there is to be progress in theological understanding, and in the practical application of the faith. Furthermore it can be argued that willingness to take this risk shows a fundamental confidence in Catholic truth and in the capacity of this truth to survive in the free market of ideas. One may recall the words of St Irenaeus about the false teachers of his day: *Adversus eos victoria est sententiae eorum manifestatio.*[8]

Where we have confidence in one another and in God, where we have patience, mutual forbearance, and a profound conviction that the truth of God is something larger than any of our ideas of it, then the way opens up to new and reconciling ways of understanding. The whole development of the theological dialogue in the last fifty years witnesses to this.

Furthermore as Anglicans we share a conviction that the only unity of faith which is lasting and valuable is a *free* unity of faith. A uniformity, whether in belief or in practice, which is imposed by some external, coercive authority is a stifling thing, in the end destructive of the life it is meant to safeguard. There should be, of course, a proper respect for authorities in the Church, and a true concern not to disturb unnecessarily the faith and devotion of the mass of the people of God. But this is something different from a blind submission to a superior authority. In the deepest part of our tradition we can perceive that it is only in the power of God the Holy Spirit that the free unity is to be found, in which the Gospel can be proclaimed to men of every culture and every situation.

> The work begun by Christ was to be carried on by those who had learned from him; but it was to be carried on under every variation of time and place and circumstance. Each act of true apostleship would lead further away from the original external conditions, and render more indispensable the interpretative office of the Spirit.

As the Church obeys the command to preach the Gospel to every creature, so the necessity for the Spirit's work of interpretation becomes ever more urgent. But this work of the Spirit by which the Church's tradition and proclamation are constantly made new, will never draw men away from the unchanging truth of Christ. In the power of the Spirit past and present, identity and development are made one. To quote F. J. A. Hort again,

> The Truth given in Christ will need from age to age the Spirit's expounding to unlock its stores; but the faith in the Spirit and in his office in the present will never loosen men from the Gospel given once for all, or draw them away from the eternal Father. . . . Standing fast in the unchanging Truth, and an endless progress in taking knowledge of it shall be indissolubly united.[9]

IV

The mission of the Church of Christ is now a planetary operation, in the sense that the Church is now in some measure present throughout mankind, in the sense that in most places it finds itself in a

minority and missionary situation, in the sense that the world
becomes ever more conscious of itself as one place. One of the
greatest limitations of our Western Churches, even in their missionary implantation beyond the Western world, is their identification
with the culture of the North American-Western European area. At
this level alone the reconciliation of the Western Churches with the
Christian East is a matter of the greatest urgency. The Eastern
Orthodox Church with its capacity to penetrate deeply into the life
of very diverse peoples, Greek and Syrian, Slavonic and Romanian,
has something special to teach us here. And if a reconciliation with
the Oriental Churches is brought about, they with their age-old
identification with Asia and Africa will have a further vital contribution to make, in revealing that the Christian faith is not to be
identified with any one culture or civilisation.

But the question goes deeper than that. How is the Church to
retain its identity and yet adapt itself and grow into the changing
world of the twenty-first century? Is it possible to change and yet
remain the same? Is it possible truly to remain the same unless one
changes? Will the Western Churches survive their present moods of
violent self-criticism without further schisms, or through them will
they even be able to move towards unity? In the providence of God
has Eastern Christianity with its long history of persecution and
oppression been forced back upon itself, so as to preserve, at its
heart, some secret of the inner identity of the Spirit's work through
the centuries, some essential element of the unifying aspect of the
Church's comprehensiveness? Have our Western Churches been led
out into contact with the world, in order to discover how God
himself in Christ is at work in varying ways in all the religions and
cultures of mankind, so that we have to offer an equally essential
element of diversification to the unity of the whole? Is there some
real complementarity of function between Christian East and West
at this point, something which God could show us if we would
together approach him in faith and expectation? If there is, then the
Anglican-Orthodox conversations which we are preparing might
prove to be of greater importance than we have yet recognised, and
indeed of significance for the whole Christian world, and the whole
of mankind.

NOTES

1. *The Lambeth Conference Report,* 1968, p. 140f
2. *The Greek Orthodox Theological Review,* XIII, 2
3. *The Lambeth Conference Report,* 1958, 2, 79–81
4. *The Lambeth Conference Report,* 1948, pp. 84–6
5. E. Milner-White and W. L. Knox, quoted in *The Lambeth Conference Report,* 1968, p. 141
6. *The Lambeth Conference Report,* 1968, p. 82
7. ibid.
8. John Macquarrie. *Concilium,* Vol. 4, No. 6, April, 1970
9. F. J. A. Hort, *The Way, the Truth and the Life,* pp. 19, 59

IV

THEOLOGIANS OF LOVE AND KNOWLEDGE

10

F. D. Maurice

As he lay on his death bed, F. D. Maurice was heard to be speaking about the Holy Communion, that it was 'for all nations and peoples, for men who were working', that it was women's work to teach men its meaning. His last words of all were the words of the Trinitarian blessing. A few months earlier, in speaking to his son, he had said: 'I have laid a great many addled eggs in my time . . . but I think I see a connection through the whole of my life . . . the desire for Unity and the search after Unity both in the nation and the Church has haunted me all my days.'[1] So at the end of his life the thought of unity, of the Name of the Triune God, of the gathering together of all nations in the feast of the Kingdom came back to him and showed him the meaning of his life. In this final moment he came very close to one of the greatest of his contemporaries, one from whom in that life he had been deeply and tragically divided, E. B. Pusey. Pusey, too, as he lay dying had in his mind the mystery of the Eucharist, and constantly repeated the words of administration and the words of absolution.[2] It was at the heart of that mystery of unifying love that both men had lived.

There has been of late among some writers on F. D. Maurice a call for a more critical approach. It has been said that too many of the commentators on Maurice in the last twenty-five years have been no more than admirers, their work hagiographical.[3] By starting at the unfashionable point of a man's death bed I might be thought to align myself explicitly with the hagiographers. Indeed, in a sense, I do so; not that I think we should be uncritical of Maurice's theology, nor that we should be blind to his personal failures and limitations. Rather because I cannot myself make sense of the life and work of this man except on the assumption that in some strange and startling way God made himself known through him. A saint, I take it, is not one who is faultless or infallible, but one who can be said so truly to belong to God that his whole life becomes a witness to the reality of God. In the famous words of Nathan Söderblom, 'Saints are such as show clearly and plainly in their lives and deeds and in their very being, that God lives.'[4] In such a man, thinking and praying and living come together into a remarkable unity.

It would not be surprising if the life of a man of this kind were also full of contradiction and controversy. Such a calling is easily misunderstood, even by the one who himself receives it. We cannot but feel that Maurice himself did not always know what it was that his vocation meant. 'I have laid a great many addled eggs . . .' In fact in a strange but not unprecedented way the meaning and fruitfulness of his work have begun to become apparent only in the century since his death. We might think of how his writing has proved an inspiration to men as diverse as H. H. Kelly, Charles Raven, William Temple, Richard Niebuhr or Michael Ramsey. We might think of the way in which *The Kingdom of Christ* has provided a kind of model for ecumenical thinking, not only for Anglicans but for many others. We might think of Maurice as one of the pioneer figures in that movement towards unity which, as it has gathered momentum in these last years has radically altered and is radically altering our experience and understanding of what Christendom is.

If we are to understand his significance aright, we shall need to see Maurice in a larger perspective than has been usual up to now. We shall need to see him in relation to that remarkable group of men who, in many different places and from many different backgrounds in the years between 1820 and 1850, gained a new vision of the Church as an organic, growing reality, and a new sense of the inter-relationships of the separated members of the one Christian family. One might think of Philip Schaff and J. W. Nevin at Mercersburg in Pennsylvania,[5] one might think on the other side of Christendom of Alexei Khomiakov and his friends in Russia.[6] One might think in Germany of a Catholic like Johann Adam Möhler,[7] or of a Lutheran like Wilhelm Löhe.[8] One might think in Denmark of the great but isolated figure of Nikolai Frederik Severin Grundt-vig;[9] one might think at home of Pusey and Keble and Newman. They are a very diverse group of people, but looking back from our present vantage point, at which we begin in a new way to discover how deeply all Christians are interdependent, we can also see their surprising similarities.

If we need to see Maurice on a larger canvas than that of England, so, too, we need to see him on a larger time scale than that of the nineteenth century. Again it will be one of the underlying concerns of this essay to point to Maurice's deep indebtedness to the Fathers, and particularly the Greek Fathers. It may be that one of his most important gifts to us is the way in which he lets the spirit of the Fathers come to life in mid-nineteenth-century England.

Maurice's work then is a focus of unity within the Christian tradition, both in space and time. But surely it is more than that. However hasty and inadequate we may find his discussion of the other religious traditions of mankind, at least we must honour his will to study them, his desire to break out of the parochialism of so much Christian thinking, and his longing to see the mystery of Christ in relation to the fears and hopes, the thoughts and specula-tions of men of all times and all races. Here again he is pointing us forward into ways which we are only beginning to explore.

But before we press on any further in our pursuit of these lines of thought, we must allow ourselves to be brought up sharply by a different estimate of Maurice, one which we must at least consider seriously. The fullest and most systematic study of Maurice's theo-logy so far to be published is the work of Professor Torben Christen-sen, *Logos og Inkarnation,* first published in Copenhagen in 1954, and more recently published in an English version, as *The Divine Order: A Study of F. D. Maurice's Theology.*[10]

Christensen does not see Maurice as an ecumenical prophet, a herald of unity. Rather he sees him as a brilliant but self-opinionated man, locked up in his own vision of things, and increasingly unable to enter into the position of anyone else; a man who constructed a large, impressive, tightly knit system, much more logically consis-tent than has usually been allowed which, though it contains consi-derable biblical elements, is yet in its basic structures Platonist and not biblical at all, and therefore not in the deepest sense Christian.

So categorical is this judgement that Christensen disallows the value of any comparison of Maurice's thought with that of, say, Luther, a comparison which has sometimes been made in view of Maurice's expressed admiration for the German reformer and of the apparent similarity between their thought at certain points. Furthermore, and for the same reason, he sharply discouraged the first attempts which were being made in Denmark to compare Maurice's work with that of Grundtvig.[11]

In Christensen's view, Maurice presents us with a static picture of an eternal work of immutable divine truths, mirrored by an equally static world at the human and material level. Nothing ever really happens in history. Historical events simply exemplify eternal verities. There can be no real drama of salvation and redemption. All that can happen is that men can come to know what formerly they did not know, that all things have their origin in God, and will ultimately return to unity in him.

Faced with such a presentation of Maurice's thought, it is difficult to know where to begin. In the first place we may recognise that there is a Platonic strain in Maurice's thinking, and that a theologian whose motto is often 'Become what you are' will be likely to have difficulty in expressing the radically new thing which happens in the moment of salvation. We may, recognise this without agreeing that it accounts for the whole of Maurice's theology. Then again we may remember that other Scandinavian scholars have made similar accusations against other Anglican theologians.[12] One wonders whether there is some wider problem of understanding as between Lutheran and Anglican here.

Then, again at a general level, there are considerable difficulties in Professor Christensen's case. It seems at least unlikely that a man whose whole life and ministry was given to the service of the Gospel should himself have been so mistaken as to what he was doing. The testimony of so large and so varied a company of Maurice's contemporaries who were helped by his ministry as pastor, priest and preacher is not lightly to be dismissed. It seems no less unlikely that a man whose thought has influenced such a large number of other theologians, and influenced them in such a variety of ways, should have been such a closed and systematic thinker as Christensen suggests. Is it all a misunderstanding?

Christensen himself remarks more than once on the highly biblical nature of much of Maurice's language. Is this a case where style is unrelated to content? Christensen maintains that it is, and that Maurice does not mean what he seems to be saying. His case, we may feel, is hardly made out. But there is also the question, which he does not discuss, of the strongly historical and biographical nature of much of Maurice's writing. This too seems scarcely compatible with the work of one who does not take history seriously.[13] At this point, J. W. Cox in an unpublished Cambridge thesis, the only study of Maurice's theology of a thoroughness comparable with that of Christensen, makes a criticism of the latter's work which is of decisive importance. Cox asserts that it is not that Maurice's thought is unhistorical as Christensen suggests but simply that he has a different understanding of what history is from Christensen's. For Maurice, man only truly becomes man in relation to God; an unformed mass of men only become a people, a nation, when they recognise the sovereignty of God in their affairs. History is not just a matter of the space-time continuum. Rather it is when men and nations acknowledge the action of God in their life that that life truly becomes *history*. As Cox puts it: 'the relationship between God and man is constitutive of history for Maurice.' For him, 'because the Biblical narrative has to do with men in their relations with one another and in their relation to God, it *is* history. For this reason also Biblical history is moral and metaphysical.'[14]

Neither Christensen nor anyone else is, of course, obliged to agree with Maurice at this point, but it is clearly a crucial one, not only for Maurice's understanding of history, but also for his understanding of Incarnation. Man truly becomes himself when he is going beyond himself into God. In a similar way God can really enter into history, eternal realities can be present and made known in time, without denying the specificity, the uniqueness of the moments in which what is of eternity is made known. At this point, I find it impossible to deny that Cox has understood Maurice's thought from within, while Christensen has examined it minutely but wholly from without. One of the most startling weaknesses of the latter's work is the way in which his own presuppositions seem unexamined and unconscious. He judges Maurice as a theologian partly on the basis of the kind of dialectical theology current in Protestant circles twenty years

ago, partly on the basis of what he calls the 'orthodoxy' of the
mid-nineteenth century, an orthodoxy whose main supports were a
wooden theory of biblical inerrancy as the guarantee of the oppressiveness of Christian doctrine, and an equally wooden understanding
of the after-life in terms of rewards and punishments as a guarantee
of the oppressiveness of Christian morals. In a revealing footnote
Christensen admits that Maurice might have much in common with
the Christian Platonists of earlier centuries, with the Alexandrians,
the Cappadocians and St Augustine.[15] If this is what it means to be a
Christian Platonist perhaps Maurice would not have so much demur-
red. Here at least are more respectable criteria of Christian
orthodoxy than those employed by Christensen.[16]

From what has been said it will be clear that Christensen's main
thesis seems to me to be untenable. This is not to say that his work is
without value. From so thorough and systematic a study much is to
be learned. We gain a new respect for the coherence of Maurice's
thought, for its central concepts such as the primacy of the action of
God, and the idea of an inclusive uniqueness which is worked out at
many different levels. We also gain a new understanding of the
historical circumstances of Maurice's work. If, as we should maintain in opposition to Christensen, Maurice had a strong sense of the
particularity of history and of the importance of facts, as well as a
feeling for universal patterns of meaning, we might expect to find in
his own thought distinctive marks of the period in which he lived.

We indeed find such marks. And some of them are weaknesses.
One of them is Maurice's delight in attributing historical events to
the particularities of national character. The history of the Middle
Ages, and indeed of medieval thought, tends to be read in terms of
anachronistic clashes between Celt and Teuton, Goth and Latin.
Much more important and much more limiting to his work as a
theologian is his practical ignorance of Roman Catholicism, and his
share in the common prejudices of his time. Hear him for a moment
on the influence of the priest in France, as he saw it in contemporary
French literature: 'Confessors are scattered over the land like locusts;
no house is safe from their invasions; they destroy the authority of
the husband, the father; their ranks are so close that we cannot break
through them; their influence is so secret and invisible that we
cannot grapple with it.'[17] But before we let our amazement run too

far, we may reflect that in his formative years, Maurice had probably never met a Roman Catholic face to face, and that throughout his life he is likely never to have come into personal contact with a Roman Catholic theologian of any eminence. When in *The Kingdom of Christ* he wrote about Quakers, Calvinists, Unitarians and even Lutherans, he was speaking of traditions which he knew directly, whose problems in many cases had been his own. It was far otherwise in the case of contemporary Rome or Eastern Orthodoxy.

But while in his weaknesses Maurice was a man who bore the marks of his own age, he was also a man who was acutely conscious that there had been other ages which had seen more deeply into the mystery of things than his own. He never became a captive of the temporal parochialism which has affected so much 'liberal' thinking in the last two centuries. This was one of the things which his contemporaries found so perplexing about him. Everyone knew, or thought that they knew, that the Tractarians had abandoned their own age for an earlier one. They had made an idol of the past, of an imagined golden age of the Church. There was at least some truth in the accusation.[18] But here was Mr Maurice with his concern for women's education and the state of the working classes, who yet could seriously maintain that our nineteenth century, which had invented the steamship and parliamentary democracy, might still have something to learn from men of earlier and simpler ages. How could a man so progressive be so reactionary? Consider the way in which Maurice speaks about Hooker for instance, as a man 'who knew a thousand times as much of Church controversies as any of us know—and was a better logician as well as a more devout man than I suppose any of us would pretend to be. . . .'[19] Look again at the respect with which he treats the great thinkers of the Western Middle Ages, even when he is disagreeing with them, for instance in his discussion of Erigena, Anselm and Aquinas, and you will see how deeply Maurice was a man of tradition, how much he cared about thought and the history of thought.

It would be tempting to quote at length from the second volume of *The Moral and Metaphysical Philosophy*. Let these two brief extracts suffice, the one a highly perceptive judgement of some of the later effects of Anselm's theories, the other a side remark about Aquinas, which tells us much about the way in which for Maurice thinking was inseparable from living and feeling, suffering and rejoicing, an embodied activity. 'Theology has cause to complain of Anselm for having suggested theories and arguments in connection with the Articles of the Creed, which through their plausibility and through the excellency of the writer have gained currency in the Church, till they have been adopted as essential parts of that of which they were at best only defences and explanations' (op. cit., p. 97) and 'The reader may be surprised to hear how much was accomplished in these forty-eight years. To us it is a greater surprise that anybody should have been strong enough to endure the presence and the working of such an intellect as that of Aquinas for so long a time' (ibid., p 188).

Maurice was a man of tradition, and quite specifically he was a man in whom the theology of the Fathers came to life in the Church of England for our own time. The attempt to trace in any detail his indebtedness to the Fathers has yet to be made. Since so much of his writing is occasional, taking the form of lectures, sermons, addresses, he seldom quotes directly from their works. Their influence is, however, all pervasive, and it was perhaps unfamiliarity with their method and their spirit which led Christensen to think that Maurice's theology is not Christian at all, because not 'biblical' in the particularly limited sense in which parts of modern Protestantism have defined that word. A single instance, taken almost at random, can illustrate this feature in Maurice. Preaching on the words 'Thy will be done in earth as in heaven', he finds it natural to employ the patristic interpretation of the parable of the lost sheep. The ninety and nine are the angelic hierarchies, the one stray is the race of man. 'It is the effect of sin to make us look upon ourselves as the centres of the universe; and then to look upon the perverse and miserable accidents of our condition as determining what we ourselves are; so all the manifestations of God are treated as if they were merely appropriate to those accidents. . . .'[20] We must always start from God, or if from man then from man as created and restored in Christ, not from his fallen condition.

If Maurice tends in his theology, and this is a characteristic which he shares with R. M. Benson, to see everything from the God-ward side, this is because for both of them theology is primarily something which is learned in prayer, through the transformation of the human heart and mind and will by the power of God. 'We do make prayer the utterance of the will and reason of man. We consider it their highest and most perfect utterance; that in which, and in which alone, they fully realise themselves.' It is in going beyond himself, in the loss of himself in adoration that man finds his true self. 'I could not understand worship to mean anything if I did not believe this. I should look upon it as a mere phantasy and delusion. . . . I look upon it as the greatest of realities.'[21] And this conviction was not theoretical. His wife tells us: 'Whenever he woke in the night he was always praying. And in the *very* early morning I have often pretended to be asleep lest I should disturb him. . . ,'[22]

While it is interesting to trace the influence of the Fathers on Maurice's thought, it is no less important to consider its points of resemblance to modern Catholic and Orthodox writing. I will give simply one example, the distinction between person and individual, crucial in our own time to the thought of Vladimir Lossky or Paul Evodkimov; the individual, man in his separateness, the person, man in relationship to God and to others, man in his wholeness. Here is Maurice in a letter written in the mid-nineteenth century: 'I am more and more convinced that we must not use *personal* and *individual* as synonymous words, but that in fact, we shall have most sense and a most lively realisation of our distinct personality when we cease to be individuals, and most delight to contemplate ourselves as members of one body in one Head.'[23] And here again is Maurice commenting on the catholicity of the human person, based on the catholicity of God; speaking of St Athanasius he says, 'he was I do believe, in the truest, simplest sense of the words, one of the most Catholic of men, who would have quarrelled with you about nothing, but that which he believed would rob mankind of its greatest treasure'.[24]

But if the unifying, esemplastic power of Maurice's theology is to be seen profoundly in relation to Eastern Orthodoxy, ancient and modern, it is to be seen no less in relation to some of his Western contemporaries. Here one could speak of Wilhelm Löhe of Neuendettelsau in Bavaria. Rather I turn to another great Lutheran of the nineteenth century, N. F. S. Grundtvig.

It is to the undying honour of Denmark to have produced in one century two such men as Grundtvig and Kierkegaard. Kierkegaard is the very type of the solitary, the unique, the one alone. Grundtvig

is the type of the universal man, the man for others; born thirty years
before Kierkegaard, dying twenty years after him, active throughout
his lengthy life, embracing almost every aspect of the life of his
people, educationist, poet, preacher, historian, statesman, priest. If
I am to compare him with Maurice, I should want first to compare
them as men. While Maurice was the greater thinker, Grundtvig
was in many ways the greater man, larger, less anxious, more effective, more powerful. His influence on national life was immediate. I
know of no other nineteenth-century theologian whose name would
be cited in a tourist brochure in close connection with improved
methods of pig production. Both men had a similar vision of man,
made in the image of God, and both saw that the nineteenth-century
world of 'religion' which was open neither to man nor God, and
which in the Protestantism of the time was based on a theology
which started from sin, was stunting the growth of Christian and
human life. In Grundtvig's case, as in that of Maurice, this vision of
a Christian humanism was linked with his reading of the Fathers,
and specifically Irenaeus. 'The glory of God is a living man.'

In both men there was a passion for unity, which sometimes
paradoxically involved them in violent polemic. Grundtvig's greatest prophetic utterance on the subject of unity comes in his pam-
phlet of 1823, *Kirkens Gienmaele*, The Church's Rejoinder, which
contains an attack on one of the Copenhagen professors so violent
that it led to a successful libel action.[25] But his concern for unity
extends throughout his work. It informs his tremendous activity as a
hymn-writer, both in his original hymns and in his numerous translations from Greek, Latin, English and German. His aim was to give
to the congregations of the Danish Church a body of hymns for
liturgical worship, in which something of the fullness of the Christian tradition of praise might sound out in their own language. One
finds in him, as in some of Maurice's sermons on the Prayer Book, a
wonderful sense of the way in which in the power of the Holy Spirit,
the diversity of all tongues (and both, remember, are romantic
nationalists with a great feeling for their mother tongue) is united in
a common sacrifice of praise and thanksgiving.

This unity is of course based in the unity of God with man in
Christ. In this sense both Grundtvig and Maurice are theologians of
the Incarnation. But in neither case was Incarnation seen as in

opposition to redemption and atonement. Interestingly both men felt that the ultimate battle was not so much between sin and forgiveness, as between life and death, and both delighted to use of Christ's death and resurrection the language of a victorious conflict with the evil powers, which had been familiar both to the Fathers and to Luther. Both through their whole theology develop the idea of the image and likeness, and both affirm that man only truly becomes man in so far as he is transcending himself into God. Grundtvig lived in a small nation of peasants and farmers, and it was amongst such people that his preaching found most response. There is, both in his hymns and in his sermons, a kind of transfigured earthliness, which reminds one of the gospels, when God himself appeared amongst us, more human than we have ever known how to be, and took the simple things of human life, bread and wine, the work of shepherds and sowers, the relations between fathers and sons, and made them the vehicles for heavenly truths. [26]

But if both are theologians of the Incarnation, of the restoration of man in God, still more both are theologians of the Holy Trinity. This is what makes them to be *theologians* in the strict sense of the word. Hal Koch, in an old but still valuable introduction to Grundtvig, speaks of this in connection with Grundtvig's hymns. [27] It is often said that the hymns of the Spirit, the hymns of Pentecost, are the finest of all, and in view of the comparative paucity of hymns for this feast in the West, we can understand why Grundtvig's should make so great an impression. But in his writing, Grundtvig seems able also to express something of pietism's intense devotion to the Lord and Saviour, and to sing movingly of Incarnation and redemption. And then going further back, he recaptures and transforms the eighteenth century's faith in God the Creator of all, that element of belief which the enlightenment in Europe and the Unitarians in England had maintained but mistakenly isolated. In his living presentation of the Name of the Trinity, all is restored, nothing lost. What we see in the hymns and sermons of Grundtvig, we find again, in a different style in the sermons and other writings of F. D. Maurice.

The detailed comparison of Maurice with Grundtvig is yet to be made. It promises much, not merely as an academic exercise in the juxtapostion of two very different ment, divided on many issues, yet united by a common faith and a common vision, but as a stimulus to the Christian thinker of our own day, faced with the immense problems of the unity of the Church and the unity of mankind, faced with the task of recovering a responsible attitude towards the material creation. There are few theologians of the last century who would be able to throw so much light on these problems as Maurice and Grundtvig. It may perhaps be that it will be someone neither Lutheran nor Anglican, neither Danish nor English who will best be able to interpret them to us.

At least as far as Maurice is concerned let us conclude with words from two writers, neither of them English, neither of them Anglicans, neither of them knowing anything of F. D. Maurice, but both in their understanding of the task of theology enabling us to see more deeply what its meaning was for him. The first voice is that of the disturbing, creative, nineteenth-century Russian thinker, Nikolai Fyodorov. One has only to cite some of his outstanding themes to see their affinity with Maurice. Who but a man who saw family relationships as types for all human relations, could speak of the work of redemption as 'The restoration of kinship among mankind?' Who but one, who like Maurice saw the nature of man as rooted in the very being of God, could say 'The Holy Trinity is our social programme.' If we remember the words which Maurice spoke in his last hours about the Holy Eucharist, then the following quotation from Fyodorov may seem the more remarkable. 'When the liturgy ceases to be confined to the Church and becomes the reality of everyday, then the question of the Real Presence . . . will be answered in the affirmative.'[28]

The second voice is from twentieth-century Greece, from one of the most creative and original of Greek theologians, Christos Yannaras. Speaking of the work of the late Paul Evdokimov, he says:

He brought to us afresh the possibility of theology being the vision of all things. His theology was organically linked with the whole of his life . . . he had gained this gift, by means of the painful experience of an intellectual, through study, reflection, the penetrating observation of daily life, and a rich and deep sensibility. This is why he was a true master, a genuine spiritual father. . . . He refused to reduce theology to an aspect of life, and so for him there were no hostile truths, but only fragments, scattered seeds of one unique truth, which was capable of freeing and restoring to its rightful place each fragment or grain of truth however buried under earth or refuse it might be....[29]

So it was with F. D. Maurice in the nineteenth century. For him theology was not a part, but the whole; the confession of the fullness of truth, not a truth which we maintain but a truth which maintains and upholds us. It is the confession of the name of the Father, the Son and the Holy Spirit, in which human life and all things are created, restored, fulfilled. It is that liberating knowledge, which itself brings life, whose greatest secret is that in it it is not primarily we who love and we who know, but we who are loved and we who are known, with a love and a knowledge which are eternal.

NOTES

1. *The Life of F. D. Maurice, chiefly told in his own letters,* edited by his son Frederick Maurice, 1884 Vol. II, p. 632 and p. 643
2. H. P. Liddon. *Life of E. B. Pusey,* Vol. IV, 1897, p. 385
3. See for instance H. Cunliffe-Jones, 'A New Assessment of F. D. Maurice's The Kingdom of Christ', in *The Church Quarterly,* Vol. 4, No. 1, July 1971, pp. 38–50, and Torben Christensen 'F. D. Maurice and the Contemporary Religious World', in *Studies in Church History,* Vol. III, ed, G. J. Cuming, 1966, pp. 69–90
4. Bengt Sundkler. *Nathan Söderblom, His Life and Work,* 1968, p. 426
5. *The Mercersburg Theology,* ed. J. H. Nichols, 1966
6. See e.g. A. Gratieux. *A. S. Khomiakov et le Mouvement Slavophile,* 1939
7. See e.g. E. Vermeil. *J. A. Möhler et l'Ecole Catholique de Tubingue,* 1913
8. The works of Wilhelm Löhe have been republished since the war by K. Ganzert. For a brief account see *Zeugnis für die Einheit,* Vol. I, ed. H. E. Jaeger
9. No adequate introduction to Grundtvig's life and work is readily available in English. P. G. Lindhart's *Grundtvig, an Introduction,* London 1951, is too much involved in purely Danish issues to be altogether satisfactory
10. Torben Christensen. *Logos og Inkarnation, En Studie i. F. D. Maurice's Teologi,* Copenhagen 1954
11. See for instance his criticism of the treatment of this subject in Regin Prenter's great dogmatic, *Skabelse og Genloesning,* op. cit. p. 467. In the second revised edition of Prenter's work published in 1955 all reference to Maurice is removed
12. See for instance J. Carpenter, *Gore, a Study in Liberal Catholicism,* pp. 11–12 for an account of the Swedish scholar Ragnar Ekström's treatment of Gore
13. On this see the remarks of John Coulson in *Newman and the Common Tradition,* 1970, p. 190
14. J. W. Cox. *God Manifesting Himself,* an unpublished doctoral thesis in the Cambridge University Library, p. 87. A reading of Cox's work, which cer-

tainly deserves to be published in conjunction with a study of Coleridge such as Owen Barfield's *What Coleridge Thought*, 1972, would do much to establish the deep indebtedness of Maurice to S.T.C. and at the same time help to dispel a good many misunderstandings about their resemblances

15. Christensen, op. cit., p. 64 n. 74
16. Part of the difficulty in making a just assessment of Christensen's work lies in its combination of apparently contradictory qualities. His exposition of his thesis is lucid and coherent. His knowledge of Maurice's work is detailed and thorough, revealing at times important insights into the strengths and limitations of his thought. Yet at the same time there appear startling examples of lack of theological sensitivity and judgement. One such example is to be found, for instance, in the discussion of the Evangelical and Tractarian positions on justification (pp. 91–2). Another is the disproportionate weight given to J. H. Rigg's critique. For a more just estimate of Rigg's stature, the more devastating for being neither unfriendly nor unsympathetic, see Gordon Rupp's article 'Newman through non-conformist eyes', in *The Rediscovery of Newman*, ed. John Coulson and A. M. Allchin, pp. 196–9
17. F.D.M. *The Prayer-Book*, 1966 edn., p. 19. It is to be noted that Maurice bases this view on 'The modern literature of France'
18. But that it stands in need of qualification would be suggested by many things, not least the teaching of R. M. Benson, the founder of Cowley. See A. M. Allchin, *The Spirit and the Word*, 1963, pp. 25–31
19. See the passage from F. D. Maurice, *The Faith of the Liturgy and the Thirty-Nine Articles*, quoted in W. Merlin Davies, *An Introduction to F. D. Maurice's Theology*, 1964, p. 196
20. F.D.M. *The Lord's Prayer, Nine Sermons preached in the Chapel of Lincoln's Inn*, 1848, p. 48
21. F.D.M. *The Kingdom of Christ*, Vol. II, p. 22. The whole of this passage should be read in conjunction with Coleridge's concept of 'polarity'
22. *The Life*, Vol. II, p. 285, note
23. *Letters and Memorials of R. C. Trench*, Vol. I, p. 190
24. *The Life*, Vol. II, p. 147
25. Some account of *Kirkens Gienmaele* will be found in my article 'Grundtvig's Translations from the Greek', in *The Eastern Churches Quarterly*, Vol. XIV, No. 1, 1961, pp. 29–44
26. This aspect of Grundtvig's thought is well brought out in Harry Aronson, *Mänskligt och Kristet*, Stockholm 1960, one of the most helpful studies of Grundtvig's theology.
27. Hal Koch, *Grundtvig*, 1943, pp. 200f
28. A chapter of Fyodorov's work, *The Philosophy of the Common Task*, entitled 'The Restoration of Kinship among Mankind', is to be found in *Ultimate Questions: An Anthology of Modern Russian Religious Thought*, ed. Alexander Schmemann, New York 1965, pp. 175–223
29. From a contribution to the special memorial number of the French Orthodox review *Contacts*. Tome XXIII, Nos. 73–4, 1971, pp. 258–61. I have taken the liberty of replacing the name of Evdokimov by the personal pronoun in this quotation

11

Evelyn Underhill

In February 1935 Evelyn Underhill wrote to a friend: 'I have just joined the Anglo-Russian confraternity—not much use really as I am hopeless at societies and guilds and always forget their rules and prayers. But they have a magazine with good things in it, and I am most interested in the Orthodox Church.'[1]

In those days the annual conference of the Fellowship of St Alban and St Sergius was held early in the summer, and so at the end of June we find her writing again: 'I couldn't answer your letter before, being at the Anglo-Russian Conference where one was kept very much on the run. It was thrilling and the Orthodox services were quite unimaginably lovely.'[2] The contacts made at the Conference were evidently followed up. Evelyn Underhill took advantage of her opportunities of attending the Orthodox Liturgy when at home in London. So a short while later she writes to another correspondent: 'This morning was so queer. A very grimy and sordid Presbyterian mission hall in a mews over a garage, where the Russians are allowed once a fortnight to have the Liturgy. A very stage property ikonostasis and a few modern ikons. A dirty floor to kneel on and a form along the wall. . . . And in this two superb old priests and a deacon, clouds of incense and, at the Anaphora, an overwhelming supernatural impression.'[3]

I

Who was this woman whose first contact with the Orthodox impressed her so deeply, and how was it that in a brief space of time she made such an impression on the life of the Fellowship? Dying in the early years of the war, in 1941, she cannot have attended its conference more than three or four times; yet without question she was one of the Anglicans, with Bishop Walter Frere, who most deeply influenced its earlier years. In 1935 Evelyn Underhill was 60, well known both as a scholarly and as a popular writer on Christian spirituality, much admired and respected as a conductor of retreats and a spiritual guide, in contact with some of the best writers and theologians of her day.

At the time of her death, T. S. Eliot wrote in the draft of an obituary notice:

> her studies of the great mystics had the inspiration not primarily of a scholar or the champion of forgotten genius, but of a consciousness of the grievous need of the contemplative element in the modern world . . . she was always at the disposal of all who called upon her. With a lively and humorous interest in human beings, especially the young, with shrewdness and simplicity, she helped to support the spiritual life of many more than she could in her humility have been aware of aiding.[4]

This reputation survived her death, and was to last for about another fifteen or twenty years. It was during this time that I was first introduced to her writings. In or near 1946 I was given a copy of her *Letters,* a book edited and introduced by Charles Williams, and I owe more to that work than I can easily say. It provided a first introduction to the names of many of the major writers of the Christian mystical tradition; it was also a revelation of the fact that the tradition was living and practised today. It was quite clear that the interest of Evelyn Underhill and her correspondents in the subjects which they were discussing was not only theoretical. Prayer was for her and for them a matter of life and death. And what surprised me most was that the writer of these letters about Ruysbroeck and Hilton, about the prayer of quiet and the need for direction, was neither a cleric nor a monk nor a foreigner nor someone from the remote past, but a member of the Church of England living in Kensington, looking for all the world, in her photograph, like one of the elder generation of my own family.

The respect which I acquired then for Evelyn Underhill I never afterwards lost. But more generally it must be said that in the later 1950s interest in her writings waned, and what little was written about her tended to be critical if not actively hostile. The official biography written by Margaret Cropper which was published in 1958, though written with evident care and love, was not a book calculated to arrest this tendency. We are, perhaps, about to see a reversal of this trend; and the publication in 1975 of a full-scale study of her life and writing by Christopher Armstrong has certainly done something to redress the balance. For Evelyn Underhill was not nearly so limited a writer as her critics have made out. The serene and wise and witty lady of the 1930s, the author of a remarkably balanced study of Christian worship published in 1936, had not arrived at her apparently untroubled position without much toil and travail, without coming into contact with some of the most difficult and most painful problems of her time. If she made an immediate contact with Father Bulgakov and his friends, it may be because, though she had not lived through a revolution, she could understand more of what it entailed than the majority of her Anglican contemporaries. The fact that at present we are living through a period of renewed interest in religious and mystical experience, is suddenly giving her writing an actuality which it has not had since her death.

Born in 1875, Evelyn Underhill was the daughter of a successful barrister, and was to become the wife of a successful barrister. All her life was to be lived, from an external point of view, in the professional and literary world of London. Her parents appear to have been, like most English people, mildly lapsed Anglicans, and though Evelyn was confirmed at school, there seem to have been no very profound religious influences in her childhood. She soon ceased to be a communicant member of the Church, and it is clear that for the first forty years of her life she had no very high opinion of the Church of England. She was, however, a serious child of intelligence and sensitivity, with a desire to think things through for herself.

What it was that awoke in her a sense of the reality of God and the nearness of the unseen world, it is difficult to say. One influence without doubt was that of Italy, which she visited summer after summer in company with her mother. As with so many northerners, the first impact of the south was unforgettable. For Evelyn it was a discovery of art and history and religion all in one; Italy and the saints of Italy always had a special place in her affections. By the first years of this century, when she was in her late twenties, it was clear that the Catholic religion was more and more attracting her to itself, and by the year 1907 she was on the point of being received into the Roman Catholic Church.

Then two things occurred to complicate matters. On 3 July 1906 she had become engaged to Hubert Stuart Moore, whom she had known since childhood, and a year later they were married. He was adamantly opposed to her becoming a Roman Catholic, and with the full agreement of her priest adviser, Robert Hugh Benson, she agreed to wait for a number of months before acting. During those months, in September 1907, Pius X issued the encyclical *Pascendi Gregis,* and in her own words, 'the modernist storm broke' in the Roman Catholic Church. Here were obstacles of a different kind to her becoming a Roman Catholic. Evelyn Underhill joined to her overwhelming sense of the reality of the spiritual world an equally demanding sense of intellectual and critical integrity, and the Roman Church, in the heat of a major theological crisis, seemed to be making demands on her which in all honesty she could not accept. Foremost among these were questions relating to the historicity of the New Testament and the authority and inspiration of the Scriptures. But we know that she was also deeply troubled by the exclusiveness with which the claims of Rome were commonly presented at the time. She found herself, like Charles Péguy in Paris at exactly the same moment, though for somewhat different reasons, living as a kind of unchurched Roman Catholic; one who like Simone Weil thirty years later was drawn to the Church with all her being, yet somehow prevented from entering it.

At this moment what did she do? Far from abandoning her quest for the experienced knowledge of God, she threw herself into the preparation of what was to be her major literary and scholarly work, the book which gained her most renown and the one which is still most widely read, *Mysticism.*

One of the virtues of Christopher Armstrong's study is that it gives us the historical context of this work, describing the very extensive, if superficial, interest in mystical, occult and religious questions which marked the London of the years before the First World War. Some indeed felt that they were in the midst of a 'mystical revival', a movement in some ways parallel to the one which was captivating St Petersburg at the same period. Evelyn Underhill was at the centre of this movement, and her major book is one of its more permanent products. It was in every sense a pioneering work, which marked a new stage in the growth of knowledge of the Christian spiritual tradition in this country.

Mysticism has as its sub-title, 'A Study in the Nature and Development of Man's Spiritual Consciousness'. It is a study of man's experience of God, understood as carried forward on the surge of an evolutionary vitalism. From a philosophical viewpoint the book owed much to Bergson, and it has some curious similarities to the work of Teilhard de Chardin. But at the same time it is an historical study, amply illustrated with quotations, of some of the greatest writers of the Christian mystical tradition, a book which has been for many an introduction to the sources.

The mystical tendencies of the period before 1914 were brought to an abrupt end by the disasters of war. For Evelyn Underhill, the years which followed seem to have been difficult ones. How to reconcile an optimistic evolutionary view of man with the horrors of trench warfare? How to reconcile her deep religious impulses with the day-to-day life of a barrister's wife? How to maintain contact with the tradition of the Church when not actually a member of it? The final question was resolved for her in about 1919 by her decision to become again a communicant member of the Church of England.

It was just at this time that she entered into a renewed relationship with Friederich von Hügel, and that he agreed to become her spiritual director. It is, I believe, a mistake to see Evelyn Underhill simply as a disciple and populariser of the ideas of the Baron. As Christopher Armstrong makes clear, some of her distinctive ideas and intuitions were formed in outline long before she met him. But there can be no doubt that it was his influence and guidance which established her firmly in that spiritual and theological position which she was to occupy for the rest of her life, and which enabled her to bring together into one the very different elements in her own make up, social and personal, intellectual, emotional and spiritual.

Through the teaching of the Roman Catholic scholar she became settled in her Anglican allegiance.

What did she learn from von Hügel? First, how to make an absolutely vital discrimination within the problems raised by the modernist crisis, which he had experienced in a way paralleled by very few Roman Catholics. Evelyn Underhill was not to be expected to accept the views on biblical inspiration and authority then dominant at Rome. There was no question of stifling the desire for enquiry and analysis. On the other hand there was to be no compromise with the position of those modernists, like Loisy, who simply denied that there was, or need be, any historical basis for Christianity at all. Von Hügel wrote in a letter to her,

> Now I am very sure that the position which holds that *some* Historical Happenings—that the non-refusedness of their historical character and the definite belief in this genuine historicalness are *essential* ingredients of every at all powerful and at all perfect religion—is true. And I am quite sure that the opposite position—the reduction of religion to a system of mere ideas, principles etc. is *profoundly* false.[5]

From the acceptance of the genuine historical element at the heart of the Gospel many consequences flow. The mystical element in religion, the element of passionate inner experience and exploration, is not the only one. There is also an historical, institutional element; there is also a liturgical and dogmatic one; and these constantly speak to us of the priority of God's being and God's acts, realities so much greater than our experiences or our response. Any fully balanced religion needs all these elements; it needs not only inwardness but also traditional social structures. It needs to be concerned with men in society, and to reach out to all creation. All this is pointed to by Evelyn Underhill herself in the preface to the revised edition of *Mysticism* which was published in 1930. Had she been writing the book at that time, she tells us, she would have stressed much more the transcendent being of God and the prevenience of his grace. She would have made more of 'the twin doctrines emphasised in all von Hügel's work, that mysticism, while an essential element in all religion, is never the whole of it, and that the antitheses commonly

made between religions of the spirit and religions of authority,
between the mystic and the community, are false. Each has need of
the other, each supports the other.'[6]

But, of course, from von Hügel, Evelyn Underhill gained much
more than deeper theological insight. She gained also profound and
penetrating guidance for the ordering of her own inner and outer
life. Above all she gained the knowledge that the heart of Christian
prayer and worship lies not in the quest for experiences however
striking, not even in man's search for God, but in the coming of
God's love to man, and man's daily giving of himself to God in
response, in all the circumstances of his life. In coming under the
guidance of von Hügel, she was meeting not only a scholar of
European eminence, but a man who was himself the disciple of one
of the greatest spiritual fathers of the nineteenth-century West, the
Abbé Huvelin. This semi-invalid priest, whose life was spent in
Paris as a preacher and a counsellor, was the spiritual father alike of
Friederich von Hügel and of Charles de Foucauld, and for that reason
alone must be reckoned one of the most influential figures in the
formation of the Christian tradition in our century. By a remarkable,
but fruitful and eminently hopeful paradox, at the very moment of
deciding to be an Anglican, Evelyn Underhill was entering into
intimate contact with some of the deepest and most creative forces in
the Roman Catholic Church.

II

I should like at this point to quote four of the pieces of advice,
'words' in the sense in which the Desert Fathers understood
'words'—liberating instructions of a spiritual father—which Huvelin gave to von Hügel when he visited him in Paris in May 1886.
They are words which von Hügel certainly passed on to his own
disciples, and they can lead us to the heart of some of the principal
concerns of Evelyn Underhill.[7]

(1) There is no more profound and dangerous enemy of Christianity than everything which makes it narrow or petty;

(2)   'The theologians sometimes make mistakes.' I should cer-
       tainly think they do. They make mistakes, and *often*. The
       sciences, man's experience of things, have made great strides
       since theology came to a halt;
(3)   The proper spirit for you is one of blessing for every creature;
(4)   Yes, there it is; no need to go further; sanctity and suffering
       are the same thing. You will do no good to others save in
       suffering and through suffering. Our Lord gained the world
       not by beautiful speeches, not by the Sermon on the mount,
       but by his blood; by his suffering on the cross.

Anything which makes Christianity narrow or petty. We might think
of this in relation to the Church. One of the reasons why Evelyn
Underhill became so convinced an Anglican was because she saw
Anglicanism not as complete in itself, but as part of a greater whole,
'a respectable suburb of the city of God', to quote her own words.
She found here a way of living an inclusive and comprehensive
Catholicism, and thus became a great pioneer of spiritual ecumen-
ism. Her book, *Worship,* gives a sympathetic account of all the major
traditions of Christian worship, Protestant as well as Catholic and
Orthodox, as though she had been able to get inside them all. We
might apply to her the words which Thomas Merton wrote in *Conjectures of a Guilty Bystander,* 'If I can unite *in myself* the thought and
devotion of Eastern and Western Christendom, the Greek and the
Latin Fathers, the Russian with the Spanish mystics, I can prepare in
myself the reunion of divided Christians. From that secret and
unspoken unity in myself can eventually come a visible and manifest
unity of all Christians.'[8] By her life and by her teaching, Evelyn
Underhill opened out the Church which she had entered, and made
it much easier for Anglicans to be at home with areas of the Christian tradition which before had been foreign to them.

The theologians sometimes make mistakes. The positions of the
theologians are not fixed and absolute; the reality of God always goes
beyond their formulations. This does not mean that their work
should not be treated with respect: we cannot do without their
efforts towards system and coherence. But it puts their work in a
better perspective. 'If there is one thing I seem to have learned',
Evelyn Underhill writes in one of her later letters, 'in the course of

my spiritual wanderings, it is the oblique nature of all religious
formulations without exception and the deep underlying unity of all
supernatural experience. This does not prevent some ways from
being better than others, and some doors from opening more easily
on to the Eternal.[9]' So she is always willing to learn, and is always
exploring further into the facts, going to history. We might see the
meaning of her own work, in making the basic texts of Christian
mysticism available, in this context. We tend to take it for granted
today that the fourteenth-century English mystics should be easily
available in paperback, that the texts of the Spanish Carmelites, or
the spiritual writers of Flanders and the Rhineland should be access-
ible to the ordinary reader. The situation was very different sixty
years ago. In writing *Mysticism,* Evelyn Underhill was constantly
breaking new ground. The tradition was simply not known. She is
one of those most directly responsible for this changed state of
affairs.

Did her vision of the development of man's spiritual consciousness
go beyond the Christian tradition? Emphatically, it did. Although
Mysticism is primarily a study of Christian spirituality, the Sufis
feature in it in a number of places. For two or three years after its
writing, she worked in close collaboration with Rabindranath Tag-
ore on the translation of his own poems and of some attributed to
Kabir. But if at any stage she was tempted towards a superficial
syncretism, her own deep spiritual intuition and the influence of von
Hügel held her back. However, in her later works, whose Christian
orthodoxy is unquestionable, non-Christian references are not
absent. *Worship,* for instance, contains a notable chapter on Jewish
worship. Evelyn Underhill was one who could make contact across
frontiers and was recognised by all kinds of people as a person who
spoke with the authority of experience as well as of learning. She
tells us of a Muslim professor who came to see her: ' . . . after various
technical questions about mysticism, he suddenly said: "You see,
Madam, for me there is really a personal question. I have not the
happiness of this experience of God, and I *cannot* live without him
any more," and tears came into his eyes. It was illuminating to
observe that the fact that he wasn't a Christian didn't make any
difference at all.'[10] For Evelyn Underhill the facts of religious
experience, not divorced from the tradition in which they occur, yet

standing in their own right, are what matter above all.

The proper spirit for you is one of blessing for every creature. Evelyn Underhill's universality of outlook might well be linked with the third of Huvelin's sayings, the spirit of blessing for every creature. But here there is a further point to note. Evelyn Underhill was by temperament attracted to the purely God-ward aspects of religion, 'the flight of the alone to the Alone'. Throughout her life there was a struggle between the vertical and the horizontal dimensions of existence. The tension features largely in her three early novels. But again it was von Hügel who helped her to see how these things could live together, to see 'the inward in the outward', not only 'the inward in the inward'. He insisted that created realities have their own rights, that she should maintain her non-religious interests and not neglect her friends, that she should undertake practical social work, visiting in the slums of North Kensington, that she should see the principle of the Incarnation at work throughout the whole of her life. So it was that, at the end, the two impulses had become one, the movement of pure adoration providing the inspiration through which all things might be seen in the light of God's glory. In one of her last public lectures, given in October 1937, she said:

> In the days that are coming, I am sure that Christianity will have to move out from the churches and chapels, or rather spread out far beyond the devotional focus of its life . . . telling the truth about God and man, and casting its transfiguring radiance on the whole of that world in which man has to live. It must, in fact, have the courage to apply its inherent sacramentation, without limitation to the whole mixed experience of humanity. . . . Only those who have learned to look at the Eternal with the disinterested loving gaze, the objective unpossessive delight of worship, who do see the stuff of common life with the light shining through it, will be able to do that.

And then, having spoken of the need for the light of God to shine out into the world, she speaks with a sudden emphasis of the meaning of worship, adoration itself.

> The spirit of worship is the very spirit of exploration. It has never

finished discovering and adoring the ever new perfections of that
which it loves. 'My beloved is like strange islands,' said St John of
the Cross, in one of his great poems. Islands in an uncharted
ocean, found by the intrepid navigators after a long and difficult
voyage, which has made great demands on faith, courage and
perseverance; islands that reveal beauties that we had never
dreamed of and a life of independent loveliness, to which our dim
everyday existence gives no clue: yet never reveal everything,
always have some unanswered questions, keep their ultimate secret still. [11]

All this is very beautiful. But is it not a trifle cosy, a bit too
comfortable? The South Kensington lady with her mystical interests
and her devoted friends and her cats, is this the stuff of real Christian
faith and prayer? Can this stand up to the strains and stresses of the
twentieth century? It is here that the most damaging criticisms have
been made of Evelyn Underhill. In my view such justification as they
have is to be found not in her life nor in the substance of what she
says, but in certain aspects of her style. There are ways of putting
things, turns of phrase in her retreat addresses and her letters, above
all in her poems, which date her and fix her firmly in her own
milieu. No less than the little St Thérèse she is of her own time and
place. But it would be a very superficial reading of her work to see no
further than this, and not to penetrate to the reality which is within,
and the cost with which it was won.

*Yes, there it is; no need to go further; sanctity and suffering are the same
thing.* The words, again, are Huvelin's, but they recur more than
once in Evelyn Underhill, and in different contexts. Let us hear her
speaking of one of her favourite saints, St Francis of Assisi:

Wherever we get him really speaking his mind, he is never far
from the Cross; the underlying tension of life. 'Yes, there it is; no
need to go further,' said Huvelin. 'Sanctity and suffering are the
same thing. You will do no good to others save in suffering and
through suffering.' We draw very near the real Francis, though
not very near the popular notion of Francis, when we meditate on
these words. . . . The entire growth of Francis was towards the
point at which, as that strange phrase in his legend says, he was

'transformed by the kindling of his mind into the image of the Crucified', embracing and harmonising in one movement of self-abandoned love, the splendour of God and the deep suffering of man. That is charity, the outpouring passion of generous love at its full height, depth, breadth and width; a passion which is the earnest of eternal life, and reflects back to a metaphysical source. St Francis, says the *Fioretti* in a famous passage, offered his followers 'the chalice of life': and those who had the courage to drink it 'saw in profound contemplation the abyss of the infinite divine light'; a strange phrase for the sort of gift which the St Francis of popular sentiment . . . is supposed to have made the world. [12]

It was this same charity, 'embracing and harmonising in one movement of self-abandoned love the splendour of God and the deep suffering of man' which she herself knew, in her own measure, in her own life. This is that unifying love, of which St Maximus the Confessor teaches so profoundly, which brings together God and his creation through the restoration of man. It was through the knowledge of this suffering and this love that she received the radiance and the quiet peace which those who knew her in her latter years so often describe.

III

Such was the person who came in the summer of 1935 to her first Fellowship Conference, and made direct contact for the first time with the life of Eastern Orthodoxy. I say 'for the first time', since it is clear that before that date, wide as her knowledge of Christian spirituality was, it had not embraced the tradition of the Christian East, after the first few centuries. It is small wonder that she so quickly penetrated to the heart of what she found there, and was herself so quickly welcomed into the heart of that encounter between Christians of East and West. Reading the passages on Eastern Orthodox prayer and liturgy in *Worship,* published only one year later, one would never have guessed that their author had so lately come to know that tradition. What she says, not only about the

Eucharist and the Divine Office, but also about personal devotion, the meaning of icons, and the use of the Jesus Prayer, seems to come from a long familiarity. It is as though her meeting with Father Bulgakov, whose book *Orthodoxy* she cites in a number of places, had been a kind of crown on her lifetime's search for the fullness and simplicity of Christian truth.

It is the combination of symbolic richness with inner simplicity which seems above all to have struck her. 'Though here', she writes, 'corporate worship may seem to touch the extreme of ceremonial and dramatic expression, personal worship has never lost that free spirituality and inwardness, that first-hand evangelical quality which is a direct heritage from the primitive Church.' She comments on 'the great reserve and the great freedom which characterise the personal life of prayer in Orthodoxy', and remarks on 'the great liberty of response which exists . . . within the total Godward life of the Church'. The ideal of prayer she describes as 'a total supernatural act achieved by many means and transcending all means, as much within the span of the simplest as of the most instructed soul'. Of the Jesus Prayer itself she says:

> If the simplicity of its form be disconcerting, the doctrine which underlies it is profound. Orthodoxy is penetrated by the conviction of the need and insufficiency of man, and the nearness and transforming power of God. Therefore its truest act of personal worship will be a humble and ceaseless self-opening to that divine transforming power, which enters with Christ into the natural order to restore and deify the whole world.'[13]

It has sometimes been affirmed, by those wishing to clarify the differences between Christian East and West, that whereas in the West the saints bear the marks of Christ's wounds, in the East they shine with the glory of the Transfiguration. Without denying the existence of differences, we must affirm that the reality of the divine action is at once more complex and more consoling. In East and West alike those who belong to Christ, who are truly receptive to 'that divine transforming power', which is God's grace, bear in a multitude of ways the marks both of his death and of his resurrection. Charles Williams, in the introduction to his selection of Evelyn Underhill's letters, cites the testimony of a friend who saw her towards the end of her life:

> It was in October 1937 that I met her first—invited to tea with her in her Campden Hill Square house. She had just had one of her bad illnesses. The door of the room into which I was shown was directly behind the big arm chair in which she was sitting facing a glowing fire. As I entered she got up and turned round, looking so fragile as though 'a puff of wind might blow her away' might be literally true in her case, *but* light simply streamed from her face illuminated with a radiant smile. . . . One could not but feel consciously there and then (not on subsequent recognition or reflection) that one was in the presence of the extension of the mystery of Our Lord's Transfiguration in one of the members of His Mystical Body. I myself never saw it repeated on any later meeting though others have probably seen the same thing at other times. It told one not only of *herself,* but more of God and of the Mystical Body than all her work put together.[14]

In his recent book, Christopher Armstrong quotes the equally remarkable notes about her last weeks made by another friend.

> She had a good bit of pain and she set herself with great fortitude to face the situation. . . . She sent messages to many people asking for prayers for all sufferers, for the union of Christian Churches. She went through a good bit of pain which reached a climax when the distress seemed to be spiritual rather than physical. She was very strange and we thought she was dying. The next morning she became radiantly happy and remained all day in an ecstasy of triumph; from what she said she knew that something has been accomplished and the sufferers would not be disappointed. She was rejoicing in God and Christ in a way which was very different from her normally rather austere devotion. She fell asleep very peacefully.[15]

The vehement, passionate temperament which had been with her all along, and which underlay the quiet surface of her life, was with her to the end; her offering taken and transformed in the one offering of

her Lord, her death no less than her life humbly open to that divine
transforming power which lifts up all sufferers, healing what is
wounded, and constantly at work making up what is lacking
through all the Churches of God.

NOTES

1. *The Letters of Evelyn Underhill*, ed. Charles Williams, p. 243. The Fellowship is
   now a fully international association of Eastern and Western Christians.
   Its magazine, *Sobornost*, is still published twice a year.
2. ibid., p. 248
3. ibid., p. 249
4. Helen Gardner. *The Composition of Four Quartets*, 1978, p. 70
5. Margaret Cropper. *Evelyn Underhill* 1958, p. 78. The texts of von Hügel's
   letters are some of the most valuable parts of this book
6. Evelyn Underhill. *Mysticism*, 12th Edition, Revised, 1930, pp. vii–x
7. The sayings are to be found in Baron Friederich von Hügel *Selected Letters*
   (1896–1924), ed. Bernard Holland, 1927, pp. 58–63
8. Thomas Merton. *Conjectures of a Guilty Bystander*, 1966, p. 12
9. *Letters*, p. 255
10. ibid., p. 251
11. Quoted in M. Cropper, op. cit., pp. 204–5
12. E. Underhill. *Mixed Pasture*, 1933, pp. 161–2
13. E. Underhill. *Worship* 1936, pp. 270–5
14. *Letters*, p. 37
15. C. J. R. Armstrong. *Evelyn Underhill* 1875–1941, 1975, p. 291

Vladimir Lossky

One of the key problems of Christian living and thinking during the next decades—if not *the* problem—will be that of tradition. Precisely because we live at a time when everywhere in Christendom the necessity for adaptation, change, radical self-questioning is being seen; when there is everywhere a revolt against a kind of 'archaism', a concern for the past as such, which for at least a century seems to have bound down much of the life of all our Churches, the present moment could easily become a moment of mere revolt, of mere reaction. We could find ourselves in a cult of the contemporary, or in a kind of concern for the future which would be in every way as sterile as the archaism which we have just abandoned; sterile because equally time-bound, and equally unable to establish a living relationship between the first century and the subsequent centuries of the Christian era. How can a faith which is rooted in the past yet be living in the present and open towards the future? How are we to distinguish between 'traditions' and 'Tradition', between the relics of earlier ages which no longer have significance for us and the living Tradition of the Gospel which is always made new with the newness of eternity, by the power of the Holy Spirit who is the giver of life?

We shall not find the answer to these questions unless we are willing to pay attention to the witness of Eastern Orthodoxy. And if we are to hear the distinctive word which Orthodoxy has to speak to us, we can hardly do better than to listen to the voice of Vladimir Lossky; one of the great and genuinely creative theologians of our century.

At first sight it might seem exaggerated and unreal to speak of Lossky in these terms. Born in St Petersburg in 1903, at the time of his death in 1958 he was little known outside the Russian Orthodox world of Paris, where he had lived for more than thirty years.[1] At that time he had published only one book, *The Mystical Theology of the Eastern Church* (French edition 1944, English translation 1957). Since his death, however, his reputation has grown steadily.

The Mystical Theology has been recognised as a classical treatment of its subject and has been translated into a number of languages, including Greek. It has also been published in Russian in the Soviet Union. Two important theological works have been published post-humously, a second study of the theological and spiritual tradition of the Greek Fathers, *The Vision of God*, 1963, and a collection of essays, called *In the Image and Likeness of God*, made by their author before his death, but not published in English until 1974. The doctoral thesis on Eckhart which he had almost completed at the time of his death has also been published, *Théologie negative et Connaissance de Dieu chez Maître Eckhart*. It is a work of profound and exact erudition.

The quantity of his published work, however, is not large. This is undoubtedly as he would have wished. In intellectual matters especially he was a perfectionist, who would be satisfied with nothing but the best. To work with him was in itself a lesson in accuracy and in the use of words. His long years of work in the history of medieval Western theology and philosophy in the preparation of his study of Eckhart had initiated him into the strictest disciplines of scientific research. He detested any suggestion that the Orthodox theological tradition was woolly or unclear. He brought to its exposition both fervour and lucidity. If, as he always maintained, the work of the theologian takes him beyond the realm of rational understanding, this never meant for him that reason and clarity could be abandoned. Quite the reverse; the way to the knowledge which lies beyond our concepts opens up through the rigour and the humility with which we are prepared to use them.

But this concern for accuracy and detail was as far removed as possible from pedantry. For him theology and life could not be separated, and his interest in life was constant and intense, 'Everything interested him,' wrote one of his sons after his death, 'with the

possible exception of sport and pornography. However, even there
he was not intransigent. If the sports were graceful, he enjoyed
them. If the pornography were talented, he accepted it as such and
laughed it off. . . . He "lived" every minute of his earthly life as only
a man who understands the significance of free will can.' In the latter
years of his life he would frequently say that he was glad he was not
'a professor of theology' (for although he taught in a great many
informal ways in Paris and elsewhere, he was not at that time on the
faculty of an established theological institution). I have sometimes
wondered whether he had been influenced by Kierkegaard's polemic
against 'the Professor'. I believe he would have found it sympathetic.
Certainly any suggestion that theology could be a subject which one
could study as one's profession, teach in one's working hours and
then leave aside would have seemed monstrous to him. 'There are
fields in which what is commonly styled 'objectivity' is only indifference, and where indifference means incomprehension,' he wrote.
Similarly any suggestion that religion could be simply one com-
partment of one's life would have been as totally unacceptable.
Whatever Bonhoeffer may have meant by his phrase 'religionless
Christianity', I have frequently thought that it could have been
applied to Vladimir Lossky. Not in the sense that he failed to be a
devout and active sharer in all the prayer and worship of the
Orthodox Church, but in the sense that there was in him no trace of
religious affectation or 'pietism', no trace of that defensiveness about
religious matters which often marks Christian people. His faith and
his life formed one whole; a whole which, while on the one side it
was deeply rooted in an amazing knowledge and love of the tradition
of the Church, on the other was open to every genuinely human
experience, in thought, in art, in common life. He was a man who
might easily have hidden himself from the twentieth century in the
work of historical scholarship, but who instead lived to the full its
demands and its achievements. A layman, married with four children, moving much in artistic and intellectual circles, himself an
exile, and living in a country which during his lifetime knew defeat
and enemy occupation, he could not escape the agonies of our time.
Not much of this is visible on the surface of his theology, but it is I
believe one of the basic reasons why it contains a word for our time
which as yet we have hardly begun to appreciate.

Like Fr George Florovsky, the other outstanding Russian theologian of this period, Lossky's thought developed in opposition to the predominant tendencies of Russian religious thinking during the previous century. A whole line of thinkers from Khomiakov down to Berdyaev and Fr S. Bulgakov had tried to work out a distinctively *Russian* Orthodoxy, and in doing so had been not a little influenced by German nineteenth-century idealism. This seemed to Lossky to involve a betrayal of the genuinely universal vocation of Orthodox theology, and of its distinctive character. For him, as for Florovsky, the heart of the Orthodox theological tradition is to be found in the Greek Fathers; and to be Orthodox meant to be faithful to the wholeness of that tradition. To be a theologian was then not to speculate about God, as a philosopher might do, or to relate what others had thought about God, in the manner of a historian of ideas; to be a theologian was oneself to come to know God, in so far as it is given to man to know him; to come to meet God in the place where God makes himself known to man, in the fullness of the tradition of the Church. Hence his theology was rooted in the past, full of the words and thoughts both of the writers of the Bible, and of the Fathers of the Church from the days of the Apostles, through the great Cappadocians, to Maximus the Confessor, Gregory Palamas, and beyond. But this highly traditional theology was at the same time living in the present, appropriated, real, the result of a decisive commitment now, which is a commitment of life.

Christian truth is not a neutral ground, it is a conquest [he wrote]. It is not enough to expound an abstract doctrine, it is not enough to *know,* here we must commit ourselves, we must have lived what we have learned, we must constantly renew this knowledge, for life is demanding and the dead doctrine of the theology text books will not be adequate to it.[2]

And in *The Mystical Theology* he could write:

There is no theology apart from experience; it is necessary to change, to become a new man. To know God one must draw near to him. No one who does not follow the path of union with God can be a theologian.[3]

This then was not only a theology of commitment in the present, but of commitment for the future, and for eternity; a theology which looked always to its fulfilment in a life and vision which would take up all the fragmentary hints and glimpses of space and time, into a splendour which could here be only guessed at.

One of the most remarkable results of a reading of *The Mystical Theology* is the way in which it can bring this vision of what theology is alive for us. To think theologically is to be prepared at every step to have our ways of thinking transformed by the renewing of our minds. To try to adapt the mysteries of God to the limits of our fallen human reasoning is the beginning of all heresy. To allow ourselves to be adapted, changed by the grace of the Holy Spirit so that we may begin to enter into some first comprehension of eternal things is the way of Orthodoxy. Dogmatic definitions then are not final and definitive statements which exhaust the being of God, they are ways in, windows which open into a world of inexhaustible richness and amazement. Like the sacraments, like icons, like particular acts of obedience to God's will (a cup of cold water given to a beggar), they are small, concrete, given ways by which God comes to meet us, and we may come to meet him. 'For Christianity is not a philosophical school for speculating about abstract concepts, but is essentially a communion of the whole man with the living God.'

In this view of theology, the personal and the corporate, tradition and experience come together in a way which is unusual in Western thinking. By the term 'Mystical Theology', Lossky did not mean a study of the pyschological states of those with a special gift for prayer, still less an enquiry into ecstasy and visions. He referred to the way in which the truth which is held and preserved by the whole Church is to be experienced and appropriated personally by each believer. Theology, the knowledge of God, is not an isolated, individual exploit in which each one acts for himself. But neither is it a fixed structure externally imposed to which the individual simply submits.

Far from being mutually opposed, theology and mysticism support and complete each other. One is impossible without the other. If the mystical experience is a personal working out of the content of the common faith, theology is an expression for the profit of all, of that which can be experienced by everyone. . . . There is, therefore, no Christian mysticism without theology; but above all there is no theology without mysticism.[4]

In this vision of theology, and indeed of life, objective and subjective, individual and community, tradition and creativity are not opposed to each other, but made one in the coming together of human freedom with the grace of the Holy Spirit. It is only in God that man is able to become himself, discover what his nature is, discover what it is to be a person and to be free.

When one comes to examine the content of this faith as it finds expression in the work of this writer, one is struck at once by the different proportion and perspective in which the various articles are viewed, as compared with what would be typical in either Protestantism or Catholicism in the West. In the only serious study of Lossky's theology so far to be published,[5] Olivier Clément has called him the theologian of the Holy Spirit and of the human person. And indeed Clément is right in singling out these themes as ones which receive a particularly full development in his writing. But in a more general view it might be said that after a reading of Lossky one is struck by the way in which the very substance of theology seems in the West to have shrunk and become desiccated. There has been such a stress on the doctrinal of redemption, on the question of *how* man is to be saved, that the whole majestic sweep of the divine and human drama from creation to restoration has somehow been lost to view. Man is being saved from sin; but who is this man and what was he made for, and what is he being restored to? Still more, who is it that saves him? For if at times one is inclined to say that Lossky's thought centres on anthropology, on the Christian understanding of man, one is always reminded that this is a theo-centric anthropology, and that it is God himself who is the goal of all our life, and that it is the revelation of the Trinity which is, 'for the Orthodox Church, the unshakeable foundation of all religious thought, of all piety, of all spiritual life, of all experience'.[6] At this basic point Lossky's thought is at one, whatever else the differences between them, with that of some of the greatest Russian thinkers of the older school, Khomyakov, Solovyov, S. L. Frank. To adore God in the utter transcendence of his unapproachable glory is not to denigrate or belittle man whom he has made. It is to show the true height and dignity of the calling of him who is called to be a partaker of that holy and divine nature.

This salvation of man which is understood in terms of union with God, deification, is always seen in a universal setting. There is no doubt that Pauline perspectives are here maintained and renewed. 'Man is not a being isolated from the rest of creation; by his very nature he is bound up with the whole of the universe, and St Paul bears witness that the whole creation awaits the future glory which will be revealed in the sons of God' (Rom. 8:18–22). This cosmic awareness has never been absent from Eastern spirituality:

> 'What is a charitable heart?', asks St Isaac the Syrian. 'It is a heart which is burning with charity for the whole of creation, for men, for the birds, for the beasts, for the demons—for all creatures. He who has such a heart cannot see or call to mind a creature without his eyes being filled with tears by reason of the immense compassion which seizes his heart; . . . That is why such a man never ceases to pray also for the animals, for the enemies of Truth, and for those who do him evil, . . . moved by the infinite pity which reigns in the hearts of those who are becoming united with God.' In his way to union with God, man in no way leaves creatures aside, but gathers together in his love the whole cosmos disordered by sin, that it may at last be transfigured by grace.[7]

It is the thought of 'the infinite pity which reigns in the hearts of those who are becoming united with God', in this passage which takes us to the centre of a theme which is vital for our whole understanding of Lossky's position. The union of man with God in Christ, and in the Spirit, is so real, so intimate that God's love, God's pity, really moves in, energises through man's love and man's pity. There is a mutual interpenetration of human and divine, which in the loving-kindness of God does not annihilate man's creaturely condition, but raises it to that communion and union with the Eternal Creator for

which in the beginning man was made. This is the work of the Holy
Spirit

> who communicates himself to persons, marking each member of
> the Church with a personal and unique relationship to the Trin-
> ity, becoming present in each person. How does this come about?
> That remains a mystery—the mystery of the self-emptying, of the
> *kenosis* of the Holy Spirit's coming into the world. . . . He remains
> unrevealed, hidden, so to speak, by the gift in order that this gift
> which He imparts may be fully ours.[8]

So to the great problem of the Reformation period, how can grace be
truly our own, and yet truly of God, Lossky brings the whole wealth
of the Orthodox doctrine of the Holy Spirit.

Here certainly is one of the keys to an understanding of his work.
Lossky was not among those who think that the question of the
Filioque is of secondary importance. For him it marked the vital and
crucial difference between Orthdoxy and Roman Catholicism. The
addition of these words to the creed marked, he believed, a grievous
distortion in the Western Church's understanding of the nature of
the living God, a subordination of the Spirit to the Son, a failure to
grasp the true meaning of the 'person' either in God or in man. The
Reformers had tried to rectify this situation, but because they had
started from false premises their efforts had been in vain. They and
their opponents were imprisoned in a common set of wholly inadequate concepts. This is a thesis which has certainly not received the
attention in the West which it deserves, either from Catholics or
Protestants. Lossky's view here has often been criticised on historical
details, and it may well be that he over-simplified certain questions,
and was too anxious to fit his data into a neat and consistent
framework. Nonetheless in its main outlines it demands our consideration and will be found to be full of illuminating suggestions for
ecumenical theology. For whether or not we attribute the development to the addition of the *Filioque* to the Creed, it is a remarkable
fact that Western theology is and has been weak in its doctrine of the
Holy Spirit, and strange to what a degree some of the most classical
controversies between Western Christians have been conducted with
scarcely any reference to the Trinitarian structure of Christian think-

ing. In particular in the doctrine of the Church, Lossky believed that the West would never again find unity or wholeness until it had restored a proper balance between the Christological and Pneumatological elements in its life and order.

This means that we must recognise not only the corporate, sacramental unity of the Church as the Body of Christ, established in the saving events of Christ's Incarnation, death and resurrection, structured around the sacraments of his presence. We must also recognise that this unity of the body is one in which the individual is not suppressed but found, or rather finds himself in true personal life, life in relationship. The Church is a unity of many persons in one common life and nature. It is the created image of the being of the uncreated Trinity; and it is the Spirit who establishes each one in his own unique being and freedom.

> The Spirit is life, movement, perpetual renewal, transformation; he inspires novelty, invention, creative initiative. He leads us to relive freely, in our own way, humble certainly but nonetheless irreplaceable, the whole divine economy; to rediscover personally the fullness which is offered to us; not to merge ourselves in the Church as in an impersonal collectivity, but to give it our own face. . . . The institutional aspect of the Church ought not to impose itself on us as an end; the sacramental life itself cannot be an end; the Church as institution, the Church as sacrament must only help us personally to meet the Living God; to speak the truth that is what the Church really is; the place, the only possible place where that meeting can take place without hindrance, the place, the only possible place of our deification.[9]

These are the words of a man whose whole life was given to the study and service of the tradition of his Church, one who was passionately Orthodox in his thinking and his feeling, unconditionally loyal to the visible Church throughout all the problems and vicissitudes of the emigration; one in whom such old and used-up terms as 'churchman' and 'layman' acquired a new life and meaning. He lived every minute of his earthly life as only a man who understands the significance of free will can. 'The only true Tradition', he held, 'is living and creative, formed by the union of human freedom with the grace of the Holy Spirit.' His life no less than his teaching spoke of the fire and light which come from such a union of man with God.

NOTES

1. His collaboration in the remarkable post-war Review *Dieu Vivant* had, it is true, made his work familiar in certain French philosophical and theological circles, and his active connection with the Fellowship of St Alban and St Sergius had made his name known in some quarters in England
2. Quoted by Olivier Clément in the special Lossky memorial number of *Messager de l'Exarchat du Patriarche russe en Europe occidentale,* Nos 30–31, 1959. p. 138
3. *op. cit.,* p. 39
4. *op. cit.,* pp. 8–9
5. In the special number of the *Messager,* already referred to. It is greatly to be hoped that Dr Rowan Williams's masterly thesis on the theology of Lossky, which can be consulted in the Bodleian Library in Oxford, will soon be published. It would greatly enlarge our understanding of the Russian theological tradition
6. *op. cit.,* p. 65
7. *ibid.,* pp. 110–16
8. *ibid.,* p. 168
9. Olivier Clément resuming Lossky's teaching in *Messager* p. 185

CONCLUSION

The essays in this book have been intended to suggest a somewhat different view of theology from that which has been customary in the West. It is a view which takes seriously the possibility that we may come to know God, and not simply know about him. It would regard many of the academic disciplines, linguistic, historical and analytical, at present often taken to *be* theology, as parts of the preparation for theology, rather than theology itself. It stresses that this knowledge is of a special character, a knowing in unknowing, in which men and women find that they are known before they know. It is a knowing in which the whole person is involved and not the intellect in isolation. It is a knowing which has a strong social and traditional dimension to it. It is personal but never merely individual. In the words which he was writing on the last evening of his life, Karl Barth, arguably the greatest Protestant theologian of our century, said: 'It is always important to listen to the Fathers who have gone before us in the faith. "For God is not a God of the dead but of the living." In him they all live—from the Apostles down to the Fathers of the day before yesterday and yesterday.'[1] Such a testimony to the value of tradition, coming from such a source, is not to be taken lightly. But this knowlege which involves us in a strong sense of our inheritance from the past, also involves us in a living commitment to the Church and to the world in our own day.

As David Jenkins insists in a work which we have already cited, this approach implies a rediscovery of the objectivity and givenness of corporate knowledge, 'a careful reconsideration of corporate and traditional knowing and of serious claims to direct awareness, given of course under differing cultural and conditioned forms, of the Mystery within which, from which and to which we might live.'[2] In this book we have made attempts at such a reconsideration. We have explored some serious claims to direct awareness of the Mystery in which we live and seen something of the interaction between those who seem to have received some such awareness and the community to which they have belonged. For it is only within the wholeness of the tradition that the vision of the mystic can be rightly understood.

> In order to enter into this knowledge it is necessary to develop a sympathy and a commitment which brings about an interpenetration, a living within the realities and a living of the realities within, between the one who contemplates or receives the knowledge and the knowledge received. This is an intellectual vision which is associated with a way of life which is a necessary preparation to the vision and a necessary accompaniment to developing in the vision. For Christians this preparation and way of life involves starting on a way which is a way of participation in God and with God. It is less like looking at an object and weighing up external evidence than like participating in a life, where the energising power is that of God who proceeds beyond any images or evidence.[3]

While it would be absurd to suggest that Anglicans had any monopoly of this way of approach to theology, it would seem as if, at least in the West, they had some special responsibility and openness towards it. Theirs is a tradition which has constantly stressed the relation between theology and prayer, which has given to worship a central place in the Church's life and which in varying ways has sought to maintain the links between the different modes of theological work. How far that tradition is flourishing today may well be questioned. At least in David Jenkins it has found a spokesman whose work is the more impressive because it is evidently produced without the slightest intention of erecting a self-consciously 'Anglican' position. It seeks to do justice both to the continuing inner tradition of Christian faith and experience, and to the unprecedented circumstances of our age which demand of us new and hitherto unforeseen responses. This whole tradition can find its own true calling only as it enters into an ever-deeper dialogue with the tradition of the Christian East.

For the theology of which we have been speaking, the evidence of hymns and prayers, of liturgy and meditation is at least as vital as that of more systematic or analytical types of reflection. No less essential is the witness of those who come to know Christ primarily through loving and compassionate service of their fellow men. This is a knowledge which is given in the Spirit, and which demands for its growth the conjunction of all the faculties of man, and of the faculties of men and women of many kinds. Mystical intuition and critical thinking are both necessary to its fullness, and both need to be combined with practical and active insight and understanding. It is in the union of love and knowledge that this conjunction can take place, and man again acquire an understanding heart and a feeling intellect.

It is in the creative power of the Spirit that this union is given. The renewal of the Christian tradition of experience and understanding of the Spirit's person and work is amongst the most urgent necessities of our day. Again at the very end of his life Karl Barth was speaking of a dream 'that someone, and perhaps a whole age might be allowed to develop a "theology of the Holy Spirit", a theology which now I can only envisage from afar as Moses once looked on the promised land.'[4] We are reminded of Bishop Westcott's prophetic remark more than a century ago, that whereas it had been given to Greece to provide the categories in which the Church had made its great classical affirmations of its faith in God the Word, it might perhaps be India which would provide the categories which will allow us to speak more fully of God the Holy Spirit.

For one thing is certain: such a renewal of theology as a way of knowing God will be inseparable from a renewal of the way of Christian prayer and the way of Christian living. When we truly speak of prayer and living, we speak always of what is unexpected and hitherto unknown. That this renewal will involve for us a new assessment of the scientific and technological society we have created seems evidently true. The outlines of that new assessment we can only just begin to glimpse. That it will lead us out into a new and fruitful interaction with the other religious traditions of mankind seems equally certain. Here perhaps we can begin to discern a little of the shape of this growing dialogue, through which we may recover much of the forgotten treasure at the heart of our own tradition. For in the breakdown of the old geographical Christendom, and in the coming together of men of many cultures and traditions in a true union of love and knowledge we begin to find more of what is meant by our faith that in Christ the whole fullness of the Godhead dwells bodily, more of what is involved in our discovery of the fullness of our humanity in him. There is much that here we are only beginning to approach, as the Holy Spirit calls us together into new ways of freedom and fulfilment.

NOTES

1. Eberhard Busch. *Karl Barth: His Life from Letters and Autobiographical Texts*, 1976, p. 496
2. David Jenkins. *The Contradition of Christianity*, 1976 p. 85
3. *ibid.*, p. 91
4. *op. cit.*, p. 494

Index